lonely 🌐 planet

POCKET
CHARLESTON
& SAVANNAH
TOP EXPERIENCES • LOCAL LIFE

T0018197

ASHLEY HARRELL, MASOVAIDA MORGAN,
REGIS ST LOUIS

Contents

Plan Your Trip

Cathedral of St John the Baptist (p115),
Savannah MEUNIERD/SHUTTERSTOCK ©

Explore Charleston

Explore Savannah

Worth a Trip

Survival Guide   147

COVID-19

We have re-checked every business in this book before publication to ensure that it is still open after the COVID-19 outbreak. However, the economic and social impacts of COVID-19 will continue to be felt long after the outbreak has been contained, and many businesses, services and events referenced in this guide may experience ongoing restrictions. Some businesses may be temporarily closed, have changed their opening hours and services, or require bookings; some unfortunately could have closed permanently. We suggest you check with venues before visiting for the latest information.

Charleston & Savannah's Top Experiences

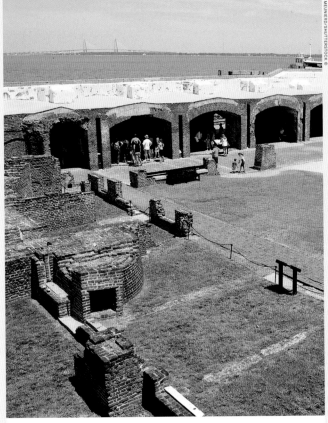

MEUNIERD/SHUTTERSTOCK ©

Explore Fort Sumter National Monument (p90)

Get outdoors at Forsyth Park (p108)

Understand the story of the South at McLeod Plantation (p78)

DARRYL BROOKS/SHUTTERSTOCK ©

J. CHRISTIAN SNEDEKER/SHUTTERSTOCK ©

Admire the Southern Gothic Necropolis of Bonaventure Cemetery (p136)

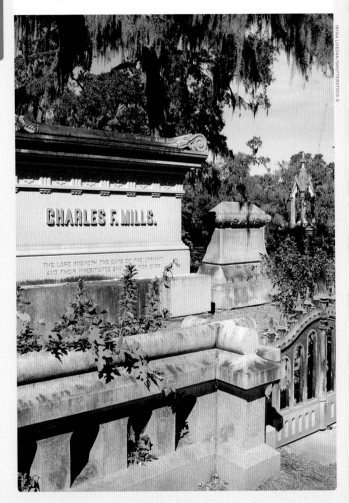

IRYNA LIVEOAK/SHUTTERSTOCK ©

CHARLES F. MILLS.

THE LORD KNOWETH THE DAYS OF THE UPRIGHT
AND THEIR INHERITANCE SHALL BE FOR EVER

Discover Wormsloe Historic Site (p144)

Educate yourself at the Old Slave Mart Museum (p32)

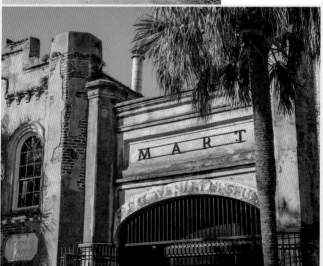

Investigate times past at the Laurel Grove Cemetery (p124)

DNDAVIS/SHUTTERSTOCK ©

Tour antebellum Aiken-Rhett House (p46)

Dining Out

Kiss your grits – you're in fine eatin' country. Lowcountry cuisine dominates the scene in both Charleston and Savannah, drawing from land (okra, field peas, rice and corn) and sea (shellfish), and heavily influenced by West/Central African traditions brought via the slave trade.

Dining Out in Charleston

Its chefs are regular contenders for James Beard awards. Its restaurants and dishes frequently get the nod from magazines like *Bon Appétit*. And with culinary roots in Europe, the Caribbean and West Africa, is it any wonder that every year millions of people pack a toothbrush just to eat in Charleston? But reading or hearing about delicious things never quite satisfies the way, say, slurping a raw oyster can. Or tearing into a fried green tomato. Or swirling the cream and sherry in a bowl of she-crab soup...

Dining Out in Savannah

Savannah is known as the 'Hostess City of the South' – and a good hostess will stuff you to the gills with all things battered and fried before sending you on your merry way. This is a city where people come to indulge in decadent, traditional Southern and soul food, but top chefs are also reimagining things with a 'New South' cuisine, where classic themes and ingredients meet innovative preparations. With Savannah's proximity to the ocean, seafood features heavily on most menus, and good grub doesn't stop at Southern staples – fans of diverse international fare can find great options, too.

BONCHAN/SHUTTERSTOCK ©

Best Restaurants

Husk Savannah Scaled-up Southern dishes made with ingredients from local purveyors. (p116)

167 Raw Hole-in-the-wall that unassumingly serves up Charleston's best seafood. (p53)

FIG Long-time Charleston foodie haven with great service and top-notch nouvelle Southern fare. (p54)

Mrs Wilkes Dining Room Rich, traditional, communal-style Southern fare in Savannah. (p116)

Best Dishes

Shrimp and Grits (pictured) Arguably the Lowcountry's most famous dish, enjoyed in varying preparations at restaurants all over town.

Lowcountry Boil Shell-on shrimp, corn on the cob, sausage and red potatoes boiled or steamed together with spices. Spread sheets of newspaper on a table, dump out the pot and get to grubbin'.

Fried Green Tomatoes Unripened tomatoes get sliced and coated with a cornmeal batter before taking a plunge into sizzling bacon fat or lard. Top 'em with pimento cheese and bacon for an extra-sinful experience, or crown a salad with a slice or two and feign being healthy.

She-Crab Soup Named for the crab roe garnish (which many restaurants leave off), this rich, creamy soup usually includes lumps of blue-crab meat, sherry and plenty of spice.

Barbecue From the Carolinas to Texas, low and slow pit-smoked protein is a US claim to fame, and Savannah and Charleston both excel at it.

Buttermilk Biscuits Whether you get 'em smothered in gravy or piled with pimento cheese, this quintessential Southern snack will have your taste buds singing.

Bar Open

The denizens of these fine cities have a famous appreciation of all things nightlife. Balmy Charleston evenings are perfect for a cool cocktail or dancing to live jazz, while Savannah's revelers often take advantage of the lax open-container regulations, bouncing from downtown watering holes to hidden haunts and bars along rollicking nightlife corridors.

Charleston by Night

Charleston may be a genteel city, but its residents are not above throwing a few back and having a good ole time. There's always something shakin' here, be it a boozy RiverDogs ball game, a highly anticipated concert at a local music venue, or swing-dance lessons at a hoppin' speakeasy. The craft-beer scene has taken off, with the best concentration of breweries in the Northern Peninsula, Mt Pleasant and North Charleston, and a brews cruise to help you hit four breweries in one. Craft distilleries are also on the rise, with two good ones right downtown.

Partying in Savannah

Savannah (pictured) knows how to have a good time – and we're not just talking the throngs of green-clad party-goers who descend upon the city for St Patrick's Day (Savannah's celebration is second only to New York City for the largest in the world). Though a modestly sized city, the nightlife turns up year-round. The watering holes are aplenty, from the tourist-frequented hubs along River St, south to the bumpin' dance clubs on Congress St, and to the locals' dives in the Victorian District. The best part? You can take boozy drinks 'to go' in plastic cups and saunter through downtown without dropping that buzz.

SEAN PAVONE/SHUTTERSTOCK ©

Best for Craft Booze in Charleston

Edmund's Oast A fancy brewpub with 64 taps and fine food like salt chicken skins, hanger steaks and hot-and-sour tilefish. (p54)

Firefly Distillery The home of America's first sweet-tea vodka, and also lots of other outrageously delicious and intoxicating liquors. (p88)

High Wire Distilling In downtown Charleston, get your tastes of small-batch gin, whiskey, vodka and amaro, right in a row. (p71)

Prohibition A speakeasy-style craft cocktail bar where you can take swing-dancing lessons. (p71)

Best for Live Music in Savannah

Savannah Smiles Dueling Pianos Croon crowd-selected favorites off rowdy River St. (p121)

El-Rocko Lounge Hip cocktail bar that regularly hosts indie, rock, soul and funk bands. (p118)

Jinx Metal, rock, alt-country and hip-hop acts blast the stacks in this gloriously grungy, small-scale venue. (p121)

House of Strut Vintage store by day and performance venue by night, where local bands jam for the hometown crowd. (p131)

Boozy Bus

Charleston Brews Cruise (📞843-860-7847; https://charlestonbrewscruise.com; 375 Meeting St; drinker/nondrinker $65/25; 🕐tours 1:30pm Sun & Tue-Thu, 12:30pm Fri & Sat) runs buses around to a rotating selection of four local breweries.

Treasure Hunt

Whether it's Lowcountry gifts, fine art and antiques, vintage garments or local farmers market products you seek, these two shopping hubs have got you covered.

Charleston

The Historic District is clogged with over-priced souvenir shops and junk markets. Head instead to King St: hit lower King for antiques, middle King for cool boutiques and upper King for trendy design and gift shops. Or try the main stretch of Broad St, dubbed 'Gallery Row.'

Savannah

West Broughton St is Savannah's pre-eminent shopping district – with both corporate and indie entities shoulder to shoulder, and all of it punctuated with a distinctly SCAD (Savannah College of Art and Design) flavor. There are also great options close to the riverfront and further south in the Victorian District.

Best Shopping in Charleston

Charleston City Market You can wander the stalls here for hours checking out local crafts and food products, such as hand-made sweetgrass. (p43; pictured)

Farmers Market Everybody comes here for local produce, homemade food and drinks, art, music, boiled peanuts and more. (p74)

Charleston Crafts Cooperative Contemporary South Carolina–made crafts, including sweetgrass baskets, hand-dyed silks and wood carvings. (p75)

Best Shopping in Savannah

ShopSCAD Pick up something unique and handmade by a local art-school student, faculty member or alum. (p119)

Books on Bay Quaint shop selling sweet vintage and antique books. (p119)

House of Strut Purveyor of thoughtfully curated vintage fashion, with local creative events in the same space. (p131)

JAMES KIRKIKIS/SHUTTERSTOCK ©

Best Food & Beverage Stores in Savannah & Charleston

Savannah Bee Company
Taste a variety of artisanal honeys at this renowned purveyor. (p121)

Tavern at Rainbow Row
America's oldest liquor store, with free weekend whiskey tastings. (p43)

Charleston Tea Plantation
There's a great gift shop here, with sets of tea bags from the only tea plantation in the US. (p84)

Goat. Sheep. Cow. North.
A gourmet cheese shop in Charleston's NoMo that triples as a cafe and wine bar. (p59)

Best Places to Shop for Art

ShopSCAD Fine art, jewelry, gifts and apparel made by Savannah College of Art and Design students and alums. (p119)

Robert Lange Studios
Charleston's most renowned contemporary art gallery. (p43)

W Hampton Brand Gallery
A gallery in Charleston's South of Broad neighborhood selling slate roof tiles with Rainbow Row painted on them in. (p43)

Worth a Trip: Bluffton

Just a quick jaunt over the Harbor River and you're in Bluffton – Hilton Head's quaint sister city, which is brimming with art studios, antebellum homes and Lowcountry charm. Artsy types will appreciate Calhoun St, which is lined with quirky galleries and shops.

Under the Radar Charleston & Savannah

Beyond the well-known historic homes in Savannah and Charleston, you can explore overlooked sites from the past and present. This can take you to surprising places from a vibrant African American cultural center to an innovative farm.

FIGNOLE PHOTOGRAPHY/SHUTTERSTOCK ©

King Tisdell Cottage

A short walk from Mother Mathilda Beasley Park, the King Tisdell Cottage (www.beachinstitute.org) is one of the best places in Savannah to delve into African American history. The Victorian cottage, built in 1896, was once the home of Sara King and Robert Tisdell, prominent members of the city's African-American entrepreneurial class in the 1920s and 1930s. You can learn about their lives and the arc of history for Blacks in Savannah and the Lowcountry in the 19th and 20th centuries. The same organization operates the Beach Institute (pictured), a cultural center set in the first school in Savannah built specifically for African-American students after Emancipation.

Weeping Time Monument

Around two miles west of Savannah's Historic District, a small park serves as a memorial to one of the largest auctions of enslaved people held in the US. In March 1859, more than 430 men, women and children were separated from their families and sold. The event is known as 'the Weeping Time' because it was said heavy rains fell ceaselessly during the two-day auction – the sky weeping over the barbarity of the event.

Fresh Future Farm

In North Charleston, a nonprofit urban farm and grocery store (www.freshfuturefarm.org) brings healthy food to an underserved neighborhood. You can visit Wednesday through Saturday.

History

In Charleston and Savannah, concerted efforts are made to keep the past in the present. In other words, everywhere you look there is a home, or a fort or even an entire neighborhood that calls a previous century to mind.

MEUNIERD/SHUTTERSTOCK ©

Best Historical Sights in Charleston

Aiken-Rhett House 'Preserved as found,' this 1820 town house showcases the lifestyle of a wealthy merchant's family and the people they enslaved. (p46)

McLeod Plantation An old Sea Island cotton plantation whose story encapsulates a larger one about slavery and emancipation in the South. (p78)

Fort Sumter National Monument See where the Civil War began, and take selfies with some old cannons. (p90)

Old Slave Mart Museum This small museum offers an important (and highly disturbing) explanation of how Charleston's prominence and wealth came from slave labor. (p32)

Middleton Place This plantation's vast gardens are the oldest in the US. (p57; pictured)

Charleston Museum The country's first museum is well organized, digestible and full of interesting artifacts and information. (p52)

Best Historical Sights in Savannah

Wormsloe Historic Site Famous for the stunning entrance to the grounds, which features a canopy of 400 live oak trees. (p144)

Fort Pulaski National monument with guided tours, a museum and trails that are great for walking and biking. (p141)

American Prohibition Museum Immersive exhibitions and storytelling shed light on prohibition in this one-of-a-kind museum. (p115)

Hauntings

Charleston and Savannah are considered by many to be two of the most haunted cities in America, and for good reason. The tumultuous histories of these cities are inextricably tied to the slave trade and the Confederacy, and countless battles were fought in and around them.

AIMEE M LEE/SHUTTERSTOCK ©

Haint Blue

While visiting Charleston and Savannah, you'll notice lots of porch ceilings painted 'haint' blue (pictured). This color was thought by the Gullah people to ward off evil 'haints' (spirits), and is also said to deter insects as well.

Spook Read

The book *Midnight in the Garden of Good and Evil* offers a good introduction to Savannah's eerie side.

Best Ways to Get Spooked in Charleston

Old South Carriage Co Offers a haunted carriage ride after dark. (p54)

Bulldog Tours Has a spooky night tour that stops at the Old City Jail, Provost Dungeon and the city's oldest graveyard. (p40)

Dock Street Theatre There have been regular sightings of ghosts in the rafters here, though some believe they're failed actors. (p42)

Poogan's Porch *Ghost Dog* is more than a Jim Jarmusch film; this place is said to be haunted by the dog it's named after. (p68)

Best Ghost Experiences in Savannah

Bonaventure Cemetery Savannah's most famous city of the dead is at once harrowing and enchanting. (p136)

Laurel Grove Cemetery This is split into two parts, with separate sections for Black and white people, and both are worth visiting for their historical significance. (p124)

Sorrel Weed House A seriously spooky mansion with grand architecture and hair-raising tours. (p114)

Romance

BONNIE DAVIDSON/SHUTTERSTOCK ©

These charming, intimate cities are the sorts where visitors tend to revel in the simple beauty of walking around. Whether you're solo or coupled up, you'll fall in love with the well-preserved history and the twisting oak trees that line the quaint avenues of these two fair cities.

Charleston is for Lovers

Charleston's most beloved 19th-century porch furnishing was the joggling board – a bouncy, wooden rocking bench that couples sat on as part of a courtship ritual. Not much has changed. Today lovers stroll cobblestone streets past historic buildings, stop to smell the blooming jasmine and enjoy long, candlelit dinners on verandas. Everywhere you turn, another blushing bride is standing on the steps of yet another enchanting church. Charleston will charm the sweat right off your brow.

Falling for Savannah

People are drawn to Savannah for its enchanting scenery, its leisurely pace of life and the endearing, soulful Savannahians who embolden everyone to let their freak flags fly. Have a wander through the Historic District and you're bound to strike up a conversation with alluring passersby, or sit for a time with someone special on the benches around the iconic fountain in Forsyth Park.

Best Romantic Experiences

Forsyth Park Home to Savannah's iconic fountain, which sits smack in the middle of a sprawling green space. (p108)

Middleton Place The vast gardens of this plantation outside Charleston are the oldest in the US. (p57; pictured)

Olde Pink House The atmosphere of this 18th-century mansion in Savannah is worth a visit alone; the food is just as good. (p117)

Zero Café + Bar Small, intimate Charleston establishment with a killer tasting menu. (p55)

The Outdoors

VINCE DOYLE/SHUTTERSTOCK ©

With bridges to islands at seemingly every turn, Charleston and Savannah are prime destinations for beachgoers, boaters and basically anyone who likes to look out over the water. Each city also offers some wonderful day trips to nearby wetlands, lowland forests and nature parks.

Getting on the Water

Without a boat friend in Savannah or Charleston, you'll need to call upon one of the local tour operators. In Savannah, a top choice is Wilderness Southeast (📞912-236-8115; www. wilderness-southeast. org; prices vary by tour & number of people), which offers wilderness adventures by motorboat and kayak. In Charleston, ring up Nature Adventures Outfitters (📞843-568-3222; www.kayakcharles tonsc.com; Shrimp Boat Lane; tours adult/child from $45/35; ⏰8am-

8pm May-Sep, hours vary rest of year). They lead local saltwater and blackwater kayak and canoe trips, as well as overnight trips down farther-flung rivers. Adventure Harbor Tours (📞843-442-9455; www. adventureharbor tours.com; 56 Ashley Point Dr; adult/child 3-12yr $55/30) is a recommended

operator for shelling trips to Morris Island.

Best Outdoor Destinations

Little Tybee Island This off-the-grid natural wonder is a draw for true adventure seekers. (p140)

Bulls Island (pictured) Offers hiking trails, shelling, alligators and a 'boneyard' beach with spooky, bare trees poking up through the sand. (p86)

Top Tips

○ Pack a bathing suit, particularly if you're visiting in the spring, summer or fall.

○ Prepare to do a lot of walking; it's the best way to experience these cities.

The Arts

Dubbed the Creative Coast, Savannah boasts a vibrant arts and design scene that's fueled by the Savannah College of Art and Design (SCAD). Meanwhile, Charleston boasts a couple of fantastic galleries and art museums, and offers a delightful art walk on the third Thursday of each month.

DIFFERENT_BRIAN/GETTY IMAGES ©

Savannah's Art Scene

SCAD is one of the finest art schools in the country, with students and faculty from far and wide. The city's art scene is also bolstered by the natives and transplants whose initiatives make the arts more inclusive and accessible. From superb museums and galleries in the Historic District to locally crafted pursuits in the Starland section, creativity is the lifeblood coursing through Savannah's artsy heart.

Charleston's Art Scene

The city's artsiest stretch, Broad St, is known as 'Gallery Row.' More than 40 galleries here and around the rest of the city participate in ArtWalk (p43). Another of the city's artistic achievements is the Charleston Step, a dramatic dance often set to ragtime jazz. It is the basis of modern swing dancing, and is thought to have been invented by African Americans living on islands near the city in the early 1900s.

Best Places to Appreciate Art

SCAD Museum of Art Contemporary art and design museum with 4500 works in its impressive permanent collection. (p114)

Redux Contemporary Art Center Charleston's contemporary art hub and event space, with three galleries and a few dozen studios. (p52)

Gibbes Museum of Art A contemporary collection in Charleston including works by local artists, with Lowcountry life as a highlight. (p66)

Telfair Academy In Savannah, the oldest public art museum in the South houses 19th- and 20th-century American and European works. (p114; pictured)

Four Perfect Days

Day 1, Charleston

OVIDIU HRUBARU/SHUTTERSTOCK ©

Spend a couple of hours meandering around Charleston's awe-inspiring **Historic District** (p31), or jump on a tour with **Charleston Footprints** (p40).

Take lunch at **Gaulart & Maliclet** (p40) or **Poogan's Porch** (p68), then visit the **Old Slave Mart Museum** (p32). Continue on for a tour of the **Nathaniel Russell House** (p38), or time-travel to the 1700s with a tour of the **Heyward-Washington House** (p38; pictured above).

Feast at **FIG** (p54) or drop into **167 Raw** (p53), then stroll the city, popping in and out of any cocktail bar that catches your eye. For a great view of the city at night, head for **Pavilion Bar** (p42) or **Rooftop at the Vendue** (p41).

Day 2, Charleston

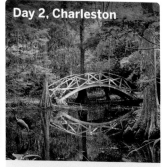

CATHYRL/SHUTTERSTOCK ©

Hit the Ashley River plantations. **Drayton Hall** (p57) features the oldest plantation house in America. **Magnolia Plantation** (p57; pictured above) offers a magnificent swamp tour. **Middleton Place** (p57) has the oldest gardens in the US, and they are exquisite.

Return to the city for lunch at Bill Murray's **Harold's Cabin** (p55). Do a lazy afternoon of craft boozing at places like **Revelry Brewery** (p56).

For dinner, stop in at **Edmund's Oast** (p54) for fine gastropub fare, or venture into **Workshop** (p58) for experimental dishes from top chefs. Attend a minor league ball game at **The Joe** (p59) or try a spooky ghost walk with **Bulldog Tours** (p40).

Day 3, Savannah

Soak in the Southern charm in Savannah's Historic District. Start at the south end of **Forsyth Park** (p108) and be sure to see the fountain and Marine Memorial. Amble up Bull St to Monterey Sq and **Mercer-Williams House** (p114).

Take a decadent Southern lunch at **Mrs Wilkes Dining Room** (p116), then walk it off heading to the **Flannery O'Connor Childhood Home** (p114) or the nearby **Cathedral of St John the Baptist** (p115; pictured above).

Dinner is upscale Southern classics at Planter's Tavern in the basement of the **Olde Pink House** (p117). Finally, catch a ghost tour at **Sorrel Weed House** (p114) and enjoy some cocktails next door at **Artillery** (p118).

Day 4, Savannah

Start the day with a dose of fine art at the **Telfair Academy** (p114) and the **Jepson Center** (p114; pictured above), then get a little retail therapy along West Broughton St.

For lunch, try a twist on classic diner favorites at **Little Duck** (p117), then check out the **American Prohibition Museum** (p115). Make your way across Bay St and down the steep staircases leading to the cobbled River St, where you can watch container ships headed in and out to sea on the Savannah River.

Enjoy inspired Southern comfort food favorites at **The Grey** (p117), a bus station turned retro-chic restaurant, then wander back across MLK Blvd and spend the night bar hopping down Congress St.

Need to Know

For detailed information, see Survival Guide p147

Cell Phones
International travelers can use local SIM cards in an unlocked smartphone or buy a cheap US phone and load it up with prepaid minutes.

Currency
US$

Languages
English, Gullah

Money
ATMs are widespread, and credit cards are accepted almost everywhere.

Time
Eastern Standard Time (GMT/UTC minus five hours)

Tipping
A 15 to 18% tip is expected in restaurants for a job well done.

Visas
Be sure you meet all ESTA visa requirements for travel to the US.

Daily Budget

Budget: Less than $165
Room at a chain motel: $135
BBQ sandwich: $10
Pint of beer: $6

Midrange: $165–275
Room at a historic hotel: $225
Bowl of shrimp and grits: $20
A well-liquor mint julep: $8

Top end: More than $275
Room at a Victorian B&B: $350
Steak dinner: $35
Craft cocktail: $15

Advance Planning

Three to nine months before Make reservations for a room at a top hotel and for top restaurants.

One month before Check online listings for upcoming theater, music and comedy performances, especially for peak months.

One week before Decide on tours and book tickets. Some require a minimum number of people, so nail down the right one in advance rather than just showing up.

Arriving in Charleston & Savannah

Most visitors arrive by air or with their own wheels. It's also possible to take a bus or a train.

✈ Charleston International Airport

Twenty minutes northwest of the city.
Shuttle $3.50-14, **Taxi** $25-30, **Bus** $2, **Rideshare** $17

✈ Savannah/Hilton Head International Airport

Twenty minutes northwest of the city.
Shuttle free-$28, **Taxi** $28, **Bus** $8

Getting Around

Bicycles, boats, buses, rental cars and taxis are all available in Savannah and Charleston.

ᨒ Bicycle

Bike-share stations, rental shops and racks are plentiful.

🚃 Bus

In Charleston, city buses cost $2 a ride, and there's also a free streetcar that makes loops from the visitor center.

In Savannah, Chatham Area Transit (www.catchacat.org) operates bio-diesel buses, including a free shuttle (the 'dot') in the Historic District.

⚓ Boat

A ferry service makes four stops around Charleston Harbor.

The free Savannah Belles Ferry (www.catchacat.org; pictured below) connects downtown with Hutchinson Island.

🚗 Car & Motorcycle

Transportation by car is the easiest and most used means of getting around.

🚕 Taxi

Ridesharing apps are usually cheaper and easier than calling or finding taxis.

Charleston Neighborhoods

East Side, NoMo & Hampton Park (p45)
Historic sights abound in these quiet neighborhoods.

Harleston Village, Upper King & Cannonborough Elliotborough (p61)
Stumble across offbeat museums and galleries as you wander.

Aiken-Rhett House ⊙

⊙ Old Slave Mart Museum

McLeod Plantation ⊙

⊙ Fort Sumter National Monument

Charleston County Sea Islands (p77)
Plantations, historic sites and lots of beaches.

South of Broad & the French Quarter (p31)
Home to many of downtown Charleston's best sights, these neighborhoods ooze charm and quiet elegance.

Savannah Neighborhoods

Beaufort & Hilton Head Island (p95)
Connect with the history and culture of colonial Beaufort before exploring 12 miles' worth of beaches on Hilton Head Island.

Historic District & Forsyth Park (p107)
The monuments, museums and grand homes of the Historic District will keep you wandering in wonder.

Forsyth Park

Bonaventure Cemetery

Laurel Grove Cemetery

Wormsloe Historic Site

East Savannah & the Islands (p135)
This stretch of coastal Savannah is a sight in and of itself.

Midtown & the Victorian District (p123)
Astounding residential architecture and a vibrant arts community.

Explore

Charleston & Savannah

Charleston

Savannah

Worth a Trip

Savannah's Historic District (p107) F11PHOTO/SHUTTERSTOCK ©

Explore ⊚

South of Broad & the French Quarter

The storybook Southern charm of the peninsula's southeastern tip cannot be exaggerated. South of Broad is simply awash in quiet elegance, and has long been considered the zenith of Charlestonian prosperity. In the French Quarter, romance emanates from cobblestone streets, and the city's oldest buildings perch among delicious restaurants and vibrant galleries.

In South of Broad the most interesting historic homes (also known as urban plantations) include the Heyward-Washington House (p38), the Nathaniel Russell House (p38) and the Edmondston-Alston House (p39). The Calhoun Mansion (p38) is postbellum, but this Gilded Age manor is the most ostentatious property in all of Charleston. The French Quarter's top attraction is the Old Slave Mart Museum (p32), and the neighborhood also lends itself to a looser itinerary of grabbing cocktail on rooftops, dipping into galleries and admiring centuries-old churches.

Getting There & Around

South of Broad and the French Quarter are easily navigated on foot, though you must watch where you're going (the sidewalks can be uneven). A couple of CARTA (p151) public bus routes serve these neighborhoods, and Charleston's bike share program Holy Spokes (p150) has stations around the area.

South of Broad & French Quarter Map on p36

Rainbow Row (p40) GORDON BELL/SHUTTERSTOCK ©

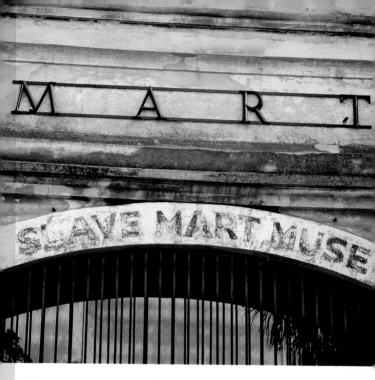

Top Experience 📷

Educate Yourself at the Old Slave Mart Museum

Formerly called Ryan's Mart, this building once housed an open-air market that auctioned African American men, women and children in the mid-1800s, the largest of 40 or so similar auction houses. South Carolina's shameful past is unraveled in text-heavy exhibits illuminating the slave experience; the few artifacts, such as leg shackles, are especially chilling.

◎ MAP P36, C3
✆ 843-958-6467
www.oldslavemart.org
6 Chalmers St
adult/child 5-17yr $8/5
🕑 9am-5pm Mon-Sat

Visiting the Museum

Before you start visiting Charleston's historic homes and plantations, and before you start walking the charming city streets, it's a good idea to educate yourself on why the area thrived before the Civil War. The short answer is: slave labor drove the economy and essentially built the city. Charleston was the nation's slave trade capital, and millions of enslaved people entered the country via the port of Charleston.

Set inside a former slave auction house known as Ryan's Mart, the Old Slave Mart Museum offers a no-holds-barred look at the business of the slave trade. Within its brick walls you'll hear the voices and the stories of enslaved people, and you'll see the shackles they wore, the whips they were beaten with and even a deed of sale for auctioned slaves.

The museum consists of just a few exhibits and text-heavy displays spread over the 1st and 2nd floors of the small building, so it'll only take an hour or two. For firsthand stories, listen to the oral recollections of former slave Elijah Green and others. In a word: haunting.

The importance of this sight looms large in the historical context of Charleston, South Carolina, the United States and beyond.

Don't Miss

o Firsthand accounts of the slave trade from freed slaves.

o A deed of sale for 235 enslaved people.

★ **Top Tips**

o Around Charleston you can find bricks with fingerprints belonging to the enslaved. Ask a docent to show you some here.

o As you wander the museum, keep in mind that you're standing in the place where traders sold human beings who were born into slavery.

✗ **Take a Break**

The museum is heavy, and many visitors come out needing to discuss the content with loved ones or to recharge a bit.

Grab a drink in the courtyard of the nearby Blind Tiger (p41).

Pick up some local moonshine at the Tavern at Rainbow Row (p43).

Walking Tour 🚶

South of Broad

You've got quite a lot of sights to hit, not to mention all the trappings of history peppered throughout the neighborhood: the old-world gas lanterns, the bricks exposed behind peeling stucco, and the 18th-century cannons jutting out of the sidewalks. This itinerary lines up the attractions and unrelenting charm in a logical way, with plenty of time for poking around palatial historic homes and peering through wrought-iron gates at flourishing gardens.

Walk Facts

Start Old Exchange & Provost Dungeon

End Four Corners of Law/ St Michael's Church (intersection of Meeting and Broad Sts)

Length 1½ miles; one hour

❶ Old Exchange & Provost Dungeon

Begin at the **Old Exchange & Provost Dungeon** (p39), where costumed guides lead tours of the dungeon where Stede Bonnet, the Gentleman Pirate, and Revolutionary War prisoners were once imprisoned.

❷ Rainbow Row

Head south to the picturesquely pastel **Rainbow Row** (p40), where you can snap your shot of these redone 1730s merchant stores that inspired the birth of the Charleston Preservation Society, along with a restoration of the entire city in the 1920s.

❸ Heyward-Washington House

On Church St, take a right and the **Heyward-Washington House** (p38), where the first president shacked up in 1791, will be on your left.

❹ Edmondston-Alston House

Head along East Battery to the Federal-style **Edmondston-Alston House** (p39), where a docent-led tour brings guests through the public rooms to view intricate woodwork and family artifacts.

❺ Battery & White Point Garden

Continue south to approach the **Battery & White Point Garden** (p40), named for the fortifications that used to line the seafront and for the mounds of oyster shells once piled over the point.

❻ Calhoun Mansion

Cut through the park and make your way north along Meeting St to the **Calhoun Mansion** (p38), a Gilded Age manor and Charleston's largest single family residence. It overflows with over-the-top souvenirs from the eccentric owner's far-flung travels.

❼ Nathaniel Russell House

Continuing north, the **Nathaniel Russell House** (p38) will appear on the left, and a tour here is worthwhile for its square-oval-rectangle footprint and free-flying spiral staircase. Don't miss the joggling board in the yard.

❽ St Michael's Church

At your final stop, the Four Corners of Law, notice **St Michael's Church** (📞843-723-0603; http://stmichaelschurch.net; 71 Broad St) on the southeast corner, representing God's law. St Michael's is the oldest church in town, and its bells have been announcing earthquakes, hurricanes, fires and attacks on the city for more than 250 years.

✕ Take a Break

Pick up a yummy sandwich at **Brown Dog Deli** (p41).

South of Broad & the French Quarter

400 m
0.2 miles

F
E
D
C
B
A

1
2
3
4

King St
Hasell St
Beaufain St
King St
Market St
Princess St
Fulton St
Jacobs Al
Pinckney St
Hayne St
Meeting St
Horlbeck Al

HISTORIC
DISTRICT

Church St
Cumberland St

West
Cemetery

St Phillips
Church

Anson St
N Market St
S Market St
Guignard St
Linguard St

ANSONBOROUGH

Bulldog
Tours

E Bay St

Cumberland St

Concord St

Waterfront
Park

9

11

13

Prioleau St
Venue Range

Queen St
State St

16

FRENCH
QUARTER

Queen St
Chalmers St

Church St

15

Charleston
Footprints

18

Washington
Square

Broad St

8

St Michaels Al

Elliott St
Broad St
Church St

10 12

Old Slave Mart
Museum

E Bay St

5 Old Exchange &
Provost Dungeon

Middle
Atlantic Wharf

19

E Elliott St

20

Boyces Wharf

Concord St

14

17

Sights

Heyward-Washington House
HISTORIC BUILDING

1 ◉ MAP P36, C5

As the name hints, this 1772 Georgian-style town house is kind of a big deal because George Washington rented it for a week, and visitors can stand in what was likely his bedroom. The owner, Thomas Heyward, Jr, was one of South Carolina's four signers of the Declaration of Independence, and it's fun to think about all the talk of revolution that must have taken place in the withdrawing room.

Enthusiasts of old-timey furnishings will appreciate the collection here, which includes a chair that belonged to General Francis Marion (the 'Swamp Fox') and the priceless Holmes bookcase, which was declared on *Antiques Roadshow* to be the most magnificent piece of furniture in America. (☏843-722-0354; www.charleston museum.org; 87 Church St; adult $12, child 13-17yr/3-12yr $10/5; ⏱10am-5pm Mon-Sat, noon-5pm Sun)

Nathaniel Russell House
HISTORIC BUILDING

2 ◉ MAP P36, B6

A spectacular, self-supporting spiral staircase is the highlight at this 1808 Federal-style house, built by a Rhode Islander, known in Charleston as 'King of the Yankees.' A meticulous ongoing restoration honors the home to the finest details, such as the 1000 sheets of 22-karat gold leaf in the withdrawing room. Twenty layers of wall paint were peeled back to uncover the original colors, and handmade, fitted, contoured rugs were imported from the UK, as originally done by the Russells.

The small but lush English garden is also notable, as is the square-oval-rectangle footprint of the home. (☏843-724-8481; www. historiccharleston.org; 51 Meeting St; adult/child 6-16yr $12/5; ⏱10am-5pm, last tour 4:30pm)

Calhoun Mansion
MUSEUM

3 ◉ MAP P36, C7

If you've ever wondered what the wealthiest, fanciest, most well-traveled hoarder's house might look like, visit the Calhoun Mansion. With 35 rooms and 24,000 sq ft, this Gilded Age, Italianate manor is Charleston's largest single family residence, and nearly every inch of it brims with the eccentric homeowner's collected furnishings, art and antiques from around the world.

Many visitors find it gaudy, but collectors often salivate, and everybody's jaws tend to drop at the sight of the Imperial Russian malachite table, the red sofa that belonged to Napoleon's brother, the hippopotamus-tooth chandelier, the samurai warrior replica that dates back to the Ming dynasty and folds into a carrying case – you get the idea. (☏843-722-8205; www.calhounmansion.net; 16 Meeting St; $17; ⏱11am-5pm)

Edmondston-Alston House

HISTORIC BUILDING

4 🎯 MAP P36, D7

Charles Edmondston built this Federal-style home in 1825 for a mere $25,000, and fell on hard times in 1837, forcing him to sell it to Charles Alston for $15,500. The Alston family upgraded the home in Greek Revival style, and it remains in their possession, with one member continuing to reside on the 3rd floor. A couple of other rooms and a carriage house out back operate as a high-end B&B.

The docent-led tour brings guests through the public rooms, which feature intricate woodwork, family artifacts and an original print of the Ordinance of Secession. The 2nd floor and piazza are ideal spots to view the harbor. (📞843-722-7171; www.edmondston alston.com; 21 E Battery; adult/child 6-16yr $12/6; 🕐1-4:30pm Sun & Mon, 10:30am-4:30pm Tue-Sat)

Old Exchange & Provost Dungeon

HISTORIC BUILDING

5 🎯 MAP P36, D4

Kids love the creepy dungeon, used as a prison for American patriots held by the British during the Revolutionary War. The cramped space sits beneath a stately Georgian Palladian customs house completed in 1771. Costumed guides lead the dungeon tours. Exhibits about the city are displayed on the upper floors.

Combination tickets with the Old Slave Mart Museum cost

Old Exchange & Provost Dungeon

MEUNIERD/SHUTTERSTOCK ©

South of Broad & the French Quarter Sights

Walking Tours

Charleston Footprints

(Map p36, B3; 843-478-4718; www.charlestonfootprints.com; 2hr tour $20) offers an excellent walking tour of historical sights led by a knowledgeable and theatrical local. **Bulldog Tours** (Map p36, C1; 843-722-8687; https://bulldogtours.com; 18 Anson St; ghost tour adult/child $25/15) also has fantastic guides for this neighborhood.

adult/child $15/8. (843-727-2165; www.oldexchange.org; 122 E Bay St; adult/7-12yr $10/5; 9am-5pm;)

Battery & White Point Garden   GARDENS

6 MAP P36, C8

The Battery is the southern tip of the Charleston Peninsula, buffered by a seawall. Stroll past cannons and statues of military heroes in the gardens, then walk the promenade and look for Fort Sumter. (cnr East Battery & Murray Blvd)

Rainbow Row   AREA

7 MAP P36, D5

With its 13 candy-colored houses, this stretch of Georgian row houses on lower E Bay St is one of the most photographed areas in Charleston. The structures date back to 1730, when they served as merchant stores on the wharf, a sketchy part of town at the time. Starting in the 1920s the buildings were restored and painted over in pastels. People dug it, and soon much of the rest of Charleston was getting a similar makeover. (83 E Bay St)

Eating

Gaulart & Maliclet   FRENCH $

8 MAP P36, B4

Ooh la la. Locals crowd around the shared tables at this tiny spot, known as 'Fast & French,' to nibble on Gallic cheeses and sausages, fondues or nightly specials ($21 to $24) that include soup, a main dish and wine. (843-577-9797; www.fastandfrenchcharleston.com; 98 Broad St; breakfast $5-11, lunch & dinner mains $11-14; 8am-4pm Mon, to 10pm Tue-Thu, to 10:30pm Fri & Sat)

Fleet Landing   SEAFOOD $$

9 MAP P36, E2

Come here for the perfect Charleston lunch: a river view, a cup of she-crab soup with a splash of sherry, and a big bowl of shrimp and grits. Housed in a former naval degaussing building on a pier, it's a convenient and scenic spot to enjoy fresh fish, a fried seafood platter or a burger after a morning of downtown exploring.

Smothered in tasso-ham gravy, the shrimp and grits here look dirty, not highfalutin, and they're our favorite version in the city. (843-722-8100; www.fleetlanding.net; 186 Concord St; lunch mains $9-24, dinner mains $13-26; 11am-3:30pm daily, 5-10pm Sun-Thu, 5-11pm Fri & Sat;)

Brown Dog Deli

SANDWICHES $

10 ⊗ MAP P36, C4

Really tasty gourmet sandwiches, packed with fresh and creative ingredients. A favorite is the Boar's Head mesquite turkey with a brie spread, bacon, sprouts, red onions and cranberry-pepper jelly. The salads and wraps are also worthwhile, and there's a second location over on the corner of Calhoun and Smith Sts. (☎843-853-8081; www.browndogdeli.com; 40 Broad St; sandwiches $8-14; ⏱11am-6pm Mon-Thu, to 8pm Fri & Sat, to 4pm Sun)

Slightly North of Broad

SOUTHERN US $$$

11 ⊗ MAP P36, D2

A tried-and-true French Quarter mainstay, with a rotating menu of Lowcountry comfort dishes reinvented with flair. Best bets include the peach salad (served with prosciutto, goat's cheese and pecans) and the duck breast. The management group behind Halls Chophouse (p69) took over this place in 2016 and left everything exactly as it was. (SNOB; ☎843-723-3424; http://snobcharleston.com; 192 E Bay St; mains $28-36; ⏱11:30am-2:30pm & 5pm-late Mon-Sat, 10:30am-2pm & 5pm-late Sun)

Drinking

Blind Tiger

PUB

12 🍺 MAP P36, C4

Opened in 1893, this cozy and atmospheric former dive, reborn in 2016 after an extensive restoration, seduces with stamped-tin ceilings, good pub grub and barrels of history. The expansive back courtyard is a popular place for a blind mule cocktail, which comes with vodka, ginger beer, lime juice and a candied ginger garnish. (www.blindtigerchs.com; 36-38 Broad St; ⏱11am-2am)

Rooftop at the Vendue

BAR

13 🍺 MAP P36, D3

This rooftop bar has sweet views of downtown and the crowds to prove it. Enjoy craft cocktails, and live music on Sundays from 2pm to 5pm. (www.thevendue.com; 23 Vendue Range; ⏱11:30am-10pm Sun-Thu, to midnight Fri & Sat)

Joggling Boards

You are not a true Charlestonian unless you have a joggling board, and South of Broad is the epicenter for this absurd but delightful porch furnishing. It consists of a 16ft plank set on rockers, and was apparently used in the early 1800s to cure rheumatoid arthritis and aid in courtship. You can find one in the yard of the Nathaniel Russell House.

Entertainment

Pavilion Bar ROOFTOP BAR

14 📍 MAP P36, D1

Complete with an infinity pool, illuminated umbrellas and stunning city views, this swanky rooftop bar tends to attract a well-heeled set. But people sometimes end up barefoot when the hotel throws plexiglass over the pool and converts it into a dance floor. (📞843-723-0500; www.marketpavilion.com; 225 E Bay St; cocktails from $9; ⏱11:30am-midnight)

Entertainment

Dock Street Theatre THEATER

15 ⭐ MAP P36, C3

Dock Street Theatre is an exquisite place to see theater. It has plenty of history – a previous iteration opened in 1736 on the same spot, becoming the first theater in America. The current performing arts center is also historic; it was built in 1809 and first occupied by the Planter's Hotel. Today it's the last (former) hotel from the antebellum period. Its Regency-style facade looks like it's straight out of New Orleans, and the wrought-iron balcony and brownstone columns channel the 1800s. It's now home to the Charleston Stage Company, and also contains the city's Cultural Affairs office and the City Gallery. (📞843-720-3968; www.charlestonstage.com; 135 Church St)

Charleston City Market

Shopping

Robert Lange Studios

ART

16 🔒 MAP P36, D3

Some of the city's best contemporary art regularly appears in this long-standing downtown gallery. Artist Nathan Durfee's experimental work is a highlight, and during **ArtWalk** (📞304-340-4253; www.artwalkcwv. com; ⏱5-8pm third Thu of the month, usually) it is a madhouse. (📞843-805-8052; http://robert langestudios.com; 2 Queen St; ⏱11am-5pm)

Charleston City Market

MARKET

17 🔒 MAP P36, C1

With more than 300 vendors hawking everything from sweetgrass baskets to piping-hot biscuits, this vibrant, open-air market is one of the nation's oldest, getting its start in 1804. The night market is held in the same space and runs from April to December, displaying the wares of more than 100 local artists and craftspeople. (📞843-937-0920; www.thecharlestoncity market.com; 188 Meeting St; ⏱day market 9:30am-6pm year-round, night market 6:30-10:30pm Fri & Sat Apr-Dec)

National Register of Historic Places 📖

There are 190 properties and districts in Charleston County on the National Register of Historic Places, the federal government's official list of places deemed worthy of preservation.

Shops of Historic Charleston Foundation

GIFTS & SOUVENIRS

18 🔒 MAP P36, B3

This place showcases jewelry, home furnishings and furniture inspired by the city's historic homes. (📞843-724-8484; www.historic charleston.org; 108 Meeting St; ⏱9am-6pm Mon-Sat, noon-5pm Sun)

Tavern at Rainbow Row

ALCOHOL

19 🔒 MAP P36, D4

America's oldest liquor store has been going since 1686. There are free tastings of local whiskey and moonshine on weekends. (📞843-722-4800; www.charlestonspirits.com; 120 E Bay St; ⏱10am-7pm Mon-Sat)

W Hampton Brand Gallery

ARTS & CRAFTS

20 🔒 MAP P36, D4

An excellent place to unearth unique souvenirs and gifts, such as likenesses of the homes of Rainbow Row, painted on reclaimed slate roof tiles. (📞843-327-6282; 114 E Bay St; ⏱9am-2pm Thu-Mon)

Explore ◈

East Side, NoMo & Hampton Park

Away from most of the tourist hubbub, the northern and eastern stretches of Charleston are fairly quiet, with a few noteworthy attractions. The East Side features a number of top restaurants, some off-the-beaten-track inns and a jumping-off point for Fort Sumter (p90). NoMo (North Morrison) was once industrial but has more recently attracted some tech companies and decent restaurants. Hampton Park, while primarily residential, offers expansive green spaces and some hyper-local cafes and breweries.

Most of the must-see sights in these neighborhoods are clustered on the East Side and tend to be historical in nature (the Aiken-Rhett House (p46), the Charleston Museum (p52) and the Joseph Manigault House (p52) are all top notch). The South Carolina Aquarium (p52) is great for kids. The Hampton Park area offers less-visited sights including the Citadel (p53) and Hampton Park (p52).

Getting There & Around

Walking these neighborhoods is possible, but some attractions are a bit spread out, making wheels more convenient. A couple of public bus routes run here, and the water taxi connects Aquarium Wharf on the East Side to Patriot's Point, Charleston Harbor Resort and Waterfront Park. Charleston's bike-share program has stations around the area.

East Side, NoMo & Hampton Park Map on p50

Hampton Park (p52) CVANDYKE/SHUTTERSTOCK ©

Top Experience 📷
Tour Antebellum Aiken-Rhett House

The only surviving urban town-house complex, this 1820 abode gives a fascinating glimpse into antebellum life on a 45-minute self-guided audio tour. The role of slaves is emphasized and visitors wander into their dorm-style quarters before moving on to the lifestyle of the rich and famous. The Historic Charleston Foundation has conserved but not restored the home, so you get the peeling Parisian wallpaper and all.

◎ MAP P50, F4

📞 843-723-1159

www.historiccharleston.
org

48 Elizabeth St

adult/child 6-16yr $12/5

🕙10am-5pm, last tour
4:15pm

Main House

Stepping through the ornate doors of this tangerine-colored mansion feels a bit like time-traveling to 1858. Not much has changed inside former South Carolina Governor William Aiken's home, and the collection of books, furnishings, art and architectural details, though worn, is largely intact. Some will find it a bit too *Great Expectations,* others will simply enjoy gawking at the peeling wallpaper, cracked plaster and chamber pots.

A stroll through the home offers insight into evolving architectural tastes in the first half of the 19th century. The upper floors exemplify the late Federal period with their careful woodwork and symmetrical proportions, while the main floor and marble staircase have been renovated in the Greek Revival style. The art gallery added in 1858 recalls the Victorian era.

Slave Quarters

The Aiken-Rhett House is often referred to as an urban plantation, and it's no secret that enslaved people lived and toiled away here as cooks, laundresses, footmen, seamstresses, gardeners and the like. Fourteen slaves are thought to have occupied the cramped 2nd-story quarters at the back of the home, and to have shared a communal kitchen. Careful analysis has suggested that the rooms had fireplaces and were painted in bright colors.

An archaeological dig in the property's laundry room has yielded some promising finds, including egg shells, fish scales, bottles, pottery and ceramics. The items (numbering more than 10,000 in total) offer insight into the daily lives of the enslaved, and some are on display.

Courtyard

Wandering the walled courtyard of the Aiken-Rhett House is an adventure, with a couple of key highlights.

★ **Top Tips**

○ Get a combo ticket for both the Aiken-Rhett House and the Nathaniel Russell House for $18, which saves you $6 (you have six months to visit both).

○ Store bags in free lockers while touring.

○ Pause the audio headset and linger when you feel compelled, or just turn it off and wander a while.

✕ **Take a Break**

King St is just a couple of blocks away, with plenty of snacking and drinking options.

Callie's Hot Little Biscuit (☎ 843-737-5159; http://callies biscuits.com; 476 1/2 King St; biscuit sandwiches $7; ⏱7am-2pm Mon-Fri, from 8am Sat & Sun, 10pm-2am Fri & Sat) offers the quintessential Charleston snack.

Juanita Greenberg's Nacho Royale (p68) has – you guessed it – amazing nachos.

Walking Tour 🚶

Hampton Park

With oodles of green space and the occasional neighborhood watering hole, sleepy Hampton Park is an ideal 'hood for a lazy Sunday stroll. Those that reside in the early-1900s abodes here tend to be raising children or part of the military, but many further-flung Charlestonians descend regularly to chillax in the grass, watch baseball or patronize their favorite bars.

Walk Facts
Start Revelry Brewery
End Palmetto Brewing Company
Duration Two hours

❶ Revelry Brewery

Revelry Brewery (p56) is a top spot for throwing back local craft beer on a rooftop, surrounded by locals and their dogs. Fridays and Saturdays are especially bumpin', and there's usually live music.

❷ Moe's Crosstown Tavern

Hands down the most popular sports dive in Charleston, **Moe's Crosstown Tavern** (p56) is famous for Sunday brunch, burgers and game-day festivities. Here people will treat you like you've been their friend for a decade.

❸ Hampton Park

Hampton Park (p52) is Charleston's largest green space, and it sure is pretty. Locals flock here every weekend to enjoy the gardens, Frisbee matches and wide-open expanses of controlled nature.

❹ Citadel

In its own little world, the **Citadel** (p53) offers a surprisingly attractive campus, innumerable cadets in uniform and a small museum featuring military apparel. Even if war isn't your thing, the center of the complex is mostly manicured lawns.

❺ The Joe

Otherwise known as **Joseph P Riley, Jr Park** (p59), this baseball stadium fills with RiverDogs fans in the spring and summer months. And apparently the food here is surprisingly tasty.

❻ Harold's Cabin

Bill Murray is the ultimate local, and he part-owns **Harold's Cabin** (p55), a former corner store turned hipster haunt with locally sourced grocery items, jackalope art, a restaurant and a bar.

❼ Leon's Oyster Shop

True locals do **Leon's Oyster Shop** (p54) on Saturday, and then again on Sunday. The oysters, scalloped potatoes and fried chicken are really that good. It gets bonus points for being set inside a converted old body shop.

❽ Palmetto Brewing Company

You might as well bookend your journey with breweries, and **Palmetto Brewing Company** (p57) is the place to end up. It was the city's first microbrewery and still holds a place in every Charlestonian's heart.

A **B** **C** **D**

1

WAGENER
TERRACE

12th Ave

Rutledge Ave

King St

26

See Inset

16

EAST
CENTRAL/
NORTH
MORRISON
DRIVE

Conroy St

N Nassau St

Meeting St

10th Ave

Gordon St

St Margaret St

Grove St

3
Redux
Contemporary
Art Center

Rodney Scott's
BBQ

NORTH
CENTRAL

2

Dunnemann Ave

College
Park

15

Cleveland St

Maverick St

Moultrie St

Huger St

17

King St

11

8

Hampton
Park
5

Mary Murray Dr

Ashley Ave

Congress St

Race St

Sumter St

Tracy St

Coming St

18

Line St

3

Jenkins Ave

Ave of Remembrance

6
Citadel
Campus
& Museum

Huger St

HAMPTON PARK
TERRACE

12

Mitchell
Playground

Hagood Ave

Johnson Hagood
Memorial
Stadium

WESTSIDE

Percy St

Ashe St

Rose La

4

Stoney
Field

Fishburne St

Harmon
Field

Kennedy St

Norman St

Bogard St

CANNONBOROUGH
ELLIOTBOROUGH

Rutledge Ave

Smith St

Ashley Ave

Smith St

20

Horizon St

Line St

Allway St

Ashton St

Spring St

5

Brittlebank
Park

17

Cannon St

President St

Bee St

Courtenay Dr

University
Hospital

Mill St

Bull St

Canon
Park

6

N
0 ————— 500 m
0 ————— 0.25 miles

Calhoun St

Morrison Dr

Newmarket Creek

E

F

G

H

Inset

21

Meeting St

Brigade St

9

Morrison Dr

EAST CENTRAL/
NORTH
MORRISON
DRIVE

William St

Lewis
Barbecue

N Hanover St

N Isabella
St

N Nassau St

26

0   200 m
0   0.1 miles

17

Johnson St

Hanover St

America St

Nassau St

Harris St

E Bay St

Martins
Park

Lee St

Jackson St

EASTSIDE

Lee St

Cooper St

Blake St

Aiken St

America St

Hanover St

Meeting St

Columbus St

Hampstead
Mall
Playground

Drake St

Cooper River

Spring St

Nassau St

Amherst St

Reid St

South St

Woolfe St

Mary St

Elizabeth St

Aiken-Rhett
House

Charlotte St

South Carolina
Aquarium 2

Cannon St

Callie's
Hot Little
Biscuit

Wragg Sq

MAZYCK-
WRAGGBOROUGH

Fort Sumter
Boat Tour

King St

St Philip St

Charleston 1
Museum

Joseph
Manigault House

Alexander St

Morris St

Radcliffe St

John St

4

Corning St

Hutson St

Marion
Square

Calhoun St

Laurens St

Warren St

RADCLIFFBOROUGH

Meeting St

13

Vanderhorst St

ANSONBOROUGH

Washington St

Calhoun St

George St

19

Anson St

E Bay St

College of
Charleston

HISTORIC
DISTRICT

Society St

7

Smith St

Pitt St

St Philip St

Glebe St

King St

Wentworth St

Hasell St

14

Bull St

HARLESTON
VILLAGE

10

Old South Carriage Co

Culinary Tours
of Charleston

E

F

G

H

Sights

Charleston Museum
MUSEUM

1 ⊙ MAP P50, F5

Founded in 1773, this is the country's oldest museum. It's helpful and informative if you're looking for historical background before strolling through the Historic District. Exhibits spotlight various periods of Charleston's long and storied history.

Artifacts include a whale skeleton, slave tags and the 'secession table' used for the signing of the state's secession documents. And don't miss Charleston's polar bear. (☏843-722-2996; www.charleston museum.org; 360 Meeting St; adult $12, child 13-17yr/3-12yr $10/5; ⊙9am-5pm Mon-Sat, noon-5pm Sun)

South Carolina Aquarium
AQUARIUM

2 ⊙ MAP P50, H4

A showcase of South Carolina's wildlife, with creatures hailing from the mountain forest, piedmont, salt marsh, coastal and undersea habitats. Although the facility is rather small in comparison with some of the country's more prominent aquariums, there are plenty of fish and other creatures. Noteworthy residents include otters, rattlesnakes, sharks and an albino alligator.

An upgraded sea turtle rehabilitation wing is a huge hit with both kids and adults. (☏843-577-3474; http://scaquarium.org; 100 Aquarium Wharf; adult/child $30/23; ⊙9am-5pm; ⛹)

Redux Contemporary Art Center
ARTS CENTER

3 ⊙ MAP P50, C1

A contemporary art hub and event space, with three galleries, a few dozen studios and some classrooms. (☏843-722-0697; www.reduxstudios.org; 1056 King St; ⊙10am-6pm Tue-Fri, noon-5pm Sat)

Joseph Manigault House
HISTORIC BUILDING

4 ⊙ MAP P50, F5

This three-story Federal-style house from 1803 was once the showpiece of a French Huguenot rice planter. There's a tiny neoclassical gate temple in the garden and the house is full of 19th-century furnishings from the collection of the Charleston Museum, which runs the site. (☏843-722-2996; www.charlestonmuseum. org; 350 Meeting St; adult $12, child 13-17yr/3-12yr $10/5; ⊙10am-5pm Mon-Sat, noon-5pm Sun, last tour 4:30pm)

Hampton Park
PARK

5 ⊙ MAP P50, B2

A big, awesome park that locals love for its arboreal and floral displays, fitness trail and large swaths of open space, often utilized for things like Frisbee matches. It has public restrooms and parking, and is rarely crowded. (📞843-724-7327; 30 Mary Murray Dr)

Citadel Campus & Museum
SCHOOL

6 ◎ MAP P50, A3

South Carolina's military college campus is set in historic buildings and is replete with uniformed cadets and various memorials. There's a small museum on the 3rd floor of the library that displays mostly military apparel. It also has a re-creation of historic barracks. (📞843-953-6845; www. citadel.edu/root; 171 Moultrie St; admission free; ⏰7:30am-10pm Mon-Thu, to 5pm Fri, 9am-3pm Sat, noon-10:30pm Sun)

Eating

167 Raw
SEAFOOD $$

7 ✕ MAP P50, G6

There are no reservations at this tiny hole-in-the-wall that unassumingly serves up the city's best seafood. People wait in lines down the block for the delicious lobster roll, and the tuna burger and sea-scallop po'boy are also off-the-charts toothsome. Oysters arrive fresh daily from Nantucket (where the restaurant runs its very own oyster farm), and the service is truly on point. Great wine selection, too. (📞843-579-4997; http://167raw.com/charleston; 289 E Bay St; oysters $2.75 each, mains $14-27; ⏰11am-10pm Mon-Sat)

Citadel Campus & Museum

EQROY/SHUTTERSTOCK ©

East Side, NoMo & Hampton Park Eating

Charleston Tours ⓘ

The East Side is a jumping-off point for many of the city's best tours. **Carriage tours** (Map p50, G6; ☏843-723-9712; www.oldsouthcarriage.com; 14 Anson St; adult/child $25/15; ⏱after 5:30pm), **food tours** (Map p50, G6; ☏843-727-1100; www.culinarytoursofcharleston. com; 18 Anson St; 2½-hr tour from $60) and **ghost tours** (p40) are among the most popular. The **boats for Fort Sumter National Monument** (p90) leave from Aquarium Wharf.

Leon's Oyster Shop

SOUTHERN US $

8 ✖ MAP P50, D3

In a converted old body shop reimagined as an industrial-chic eatery, Leon's is a Charleston favorite for three distinct and delicious items: oysters, fried chicken and scalloped potatoes. There is no better place to eat off a hangover, and the rosé on tap is a classy way to keep the party going. (☏843-531-6500; http:// leonsoystershop.com; 698 King St; oysters from $1, fried chicken meal $15, scalloped potatoes $5; ⏱11am-10pm)

Edmund's Oast

PUB FOOD $$

9 ✖ MAP P50, G1

Occupying a gutted former hardware store in gentrifying NoMo, Charleston's highest-brow brewpub got a fancy executive chef, Bob Cook, in 2017. The grub: Southern faves like salt chicken skins, hanger steaks and hot-and-sour tilefish. The drink pairings: 64 taps (eight devoted to cocktails, meads and sherries, and a dozen proprietary craft beers, among other craft offerings).

The menu isn't long on options but is absolutely outstanding on execution and flavors that complement the devoted craft scene here. It's named after an 18th-century rebel brewer. Call it a night! (☏843-727-1145; www.edmundsoast.com; 1081 Morrison Dr; mains $14-29, pints $6-9; ⏱4:30-10pm Mon-Thu, to 11pm Fri & Sat, 10am-10pm Sun; 📶)

FIG

SOUTHERN US $$$

10 ✖ MAP P50, G6

FIG has been a longtime foodie favorite, and it's easy to see why: welcoming staff, efficient but unrushed service and top-notch, sustainably sourced nouvelle Southern fare from James Beard Award–winner Mike Lata. The six nightly changing dishes embrace what's fresh and local from the sea and local farms and mills. FIG stands for Food is Good. And the gourmets agree.

Reservations well in advance are mandatory, but rogue solos might be able to snag a seat quickly at the communal table or bar. (☏843-805-5900; www.eatatfig. com; 232 Meeting St; mains $30-36; ⏱5-10:30pm Mon-Thu, to 11pm Fri & Sat; 📶)

Little Jack's Tavern
BURGERS $

11 ✕ MAP P50, D2

A classy neighborhood cocktail bar and restaurant, with one helluva hamburger (in 2017 *Bon Appétit* named it one of the top three burgers in America). The butter-soaked bun is toasted just right, and the oversized patty is smothered in a fantastic tangy sauce and savory fried onions. (☎843-531-6868; http://littlejackstavern.com; 710 King St; tavern burger $8; ⏰11am-10pm Sun-Thu, to 11pm Fri & Sat)

Harold's Cabin
AMERICAN $$

12 ✕ MAP P50, B3

It goes without saying that if Bill Murray is a co-owner, the place is probably dope. That's the case for this former corner store, which remains a rustic (if newly chic) neighborhood haunt offering locally sourced grocery items – and now it's also a restaurant and bar. The delicious, veggie-driven meals are largely made up of ingredients from a rooftop garden.

But yeah, the steaks and seafood are also super yum. Oh, and jackalopes abound. And there's a great brunch. And apparently you get a small discount if you wear black? (☎843-793-4440; www.haroldscabin.com; 247 Congress St; mains $8-20; ⏰11am-10pm Tue-Fri, 9am-10pm Sat & Sun; 🍸)

Zero Café + Bar
AMERICAN $$$

13 ✕ MAP P50, G5

The kitchen at the Zero George Street hotel (p149) might be diminutive, but the dining experience provided by Food Network celebrity chef Vinson Petrillo is enormously memorable. The chef assumes his diners are intrepid and sends out dainty plates of pressure-cooked octopus, ricotta gnudi (gnocchi-like dumplings) and scallop tartare. Vegetarians are well served with items like cappellacci (stuffed pasta) and rutabaga (swede).

The wine list is small, but the tasting-menu pairings are expertly curated. Cocktails and beer are

Best BBQ Spots 🍽

Maybe it's because barbecue needs a lot of room to be prepared and devoured, but the city's best meat-munching happens in expansive spaces in the northern part of town. In fact, the top two spots are within a half-mile of each other, and whether you're on team **Lewis Barbecue** (Map p50, H2; ☎843-805-9500; https://lewisbarbecue.com; 464 N Nassau St; mains $8-21; ⏰11am-10pm Tue-Sun) or team **Rodney Scott's BBQ** (Map p50, C2; ☎843-990-9535; www.rodneyscottsbbq.com; 1011 King St; mains $9-14; ⏰11am-9pm) is deeply personal.

also available (and a fine idea).
(☎843-817-7900; www.zerogeorge.
com; 0 George St; 6-course tasting
menu with wine $135 per person, $125
for veg; ⏱5-10pm Tue-Sun; ✎)

Cru Cafe   AMERICAN $$

14 ⓧ MAP P50, G6

Innovative comfort food, served
in a two-story, historic home with
a charming porch. This place is
beloved for its healthy salads and
unusual takes on local specialties,
for example, the deeply fried green
tomatoes with pork-belly croutons,
sheep's-milk feta and smoky
caramel drizzle. The General Tso's
Caesar wrap is also a winner.
(☎843-534-2434; http://crucafe.com;
18 Pinckney St; mains $10-25; ⏱11am-
3pm & 5-10pm Tue-Thu, 11am-3pm &
5-11pm Fri & Sat)

Magnolia Plantation

KIM LEWIS PHOTOGRAPHY/SHUTTERSTOCK ©

Drinking

Moe's
Crosstown Tavern   SPORTS BAR

15 🚌 MAP P50, C2

Considered Hampton Park's best
dive bar, this place fills with loyal
patrons on game days. The burgers and Sunday brunch are tasty;
the craft beer and camaraderie
are even tastier. (☎843-641-0469;
https://moescrosstowntavern.com; 714
Rutledge Ave; ⏱11am-2am Mon-Sat,
10:30am-2am Sun)

Revelry Brewery   MICROBREWERY

16 🚌 MAP P50, D1

Probably the hippest of the Northern Peninsula breweries. It's hard
to beat knocking back a few art-
fully crafted cold ones on Revelry's
fairy-lit and fire-pit-heated rooftop,
which affords expansive views all
the way to the cable-stayed Rav-
enel Bridge. The downstairs bar,
seemingly owned by the brewery's
black Lab, is 5ft from the tanks.

There's live music on Friday
and Sunday. Pets are encouraged. In 2018 an annex behind the
brewery was slated to open; it sell
bottles and cans and eventually
host events and tastings. (www.
revelrybrewingco.com; 10 Conroy St;
⏱4-10pm Mon-Thu, noon-midnight Fri
& Sat, noon-10pm Sun)

Plantations Around Charleston

Three significant plantations line the Ashley River about a 20-minute drive from downtown Charleston. All offer talks and tours concerning the role of slavery (though another, **McLeod Plantation** (p78), located on the northern shores of James Island, is the best for an eye-opening and highly important experience on that topic).

Of the three on the Ashley River, **Drayton Hall** (843-769-2600; www.draytonhall.org; 3380 Ashley River Rd; adult/child $22/10, grounds only $12; 9am-3:30pm Mon-Sat, 11am-3:30pm Sun, last tour 3pm) is the best for history buffs, as it features the oldest plantation house open to the public in America. **Magnolia Plantation** (843-571-1266; www.magnoliaplantation.com; 3550 Ashley River Rd; adult/child 6-10yr $20/10, tours $8; 8am-5:30pm Mar-Oct, to 4:30pm Nov-Feb) has great tours and wild gardens, with a Disney vibe. **Middleton Place** (843-556-6020; www.middletonplace.org; 4300 Ashley River Rd; gardens adult/child 6-13yr $28/10, house-museum tour extra $15, carriage tour $18; 9am-5pm) has the country's oldest, most elegant gardens and a fancy restaurant and hotel. You'll be hard-pressed to find the time to visit all three of these in one day, but you could squeeze in two (allow at least a couple of hours for each). Ashley River Rd is also known as SC 61, which can be reached from downtown Charleston via Hwy 17.

Also popular, **Boone Hall Plantation** (843-884-4371; www.boonehallplantation.com; 1235 Long Point Rd; adult/child 6-12yr $24/12; 8:30am-6:30pm Mon-Sat, noon-5pm Sun early Mar-Aug, shorter hours Sep-Jan) in Mt Pleasant is where celebrities tend to get married, and is a very pretty spot for tourists and families. It's 11 miles from downtown Charleston on Hwy 17N.

Palmetto Brewing Company

MICROBREWERY

17 MAP P50, D2

Charleston's first microbrewery (since Prohibition, anyway) produces four main craft beers with fresh barley malts and hops: an amber ale, a pilsner and a couple of IPAs. They've also got rotating special ales and even a 'Brose' radler (shandy). Tours are available on weekdays at 5pm, and the tap room and outdoor beer garden are lively on weekends, particularly Fridays.

In 2017 the business was sold to Catawba Brewing Company, and facility and equipment upgrades were pending at the time of research. (843-937-0903; www.palmettobrewery.com; 289 Huger St; 4-8pm Tue-Thu, noon-10pm Fri & Sat)

Booming Charleston

These days, the city of Charleston seems to be out for a joyride in a comfy, high-performance carriage. The carriage is cruising at a breakneck pace, yummy snacks and cocktails are getting passed around, and everybody wants to hop on. Sometimes, though, the carriage gets stuck in traffic. The price of the ride keeps going up, and the very people who got the carriage moving can no longer afford it.

This is, of course, a fairly ridiculous allegory to describe a Charleston that is booming economically, has a great restaurant scene and is attracting all kinds of visitors and new residents. But at the same time, that growth is causing traffic problems and gentrification.

The good news first: thanks to the meticulously preserved history and architecture, burgeoning restaurant scene and dreamy waterfront locale, Charleston is enjoying some of the finest times in its near 350-year history. The city's top industry, tourism, has been growing since 2012, with visitors lately tossing more than $20 billion at the city. In 2017 an estimated six million people showed up to see this peninsula that spans just over 100 sq miles. With all the awards the city has been raking in from top publications, the numbers are likely to continue their upward trajectory.

People are also moving to the city in sky-high numbers. US News & World Report recently identified Charleston as the 19th-fastest growing city (in terms of net migration) in the country, and new developments, restaurant openings and job opportunities have been springing up around the peninsula, particularly in the once industrial, now gentrifying area known as NoMo. Some are calling it Silicon Harbor, though, because the area is poised to become Charleston's tech hub, and interesting new businesses have already set up shop.

Although most residents can appreciate the brisket enchiladas, they're not thrilled about the congested city streets or the new hotel and condo projects. Downtown home prices have climbed steeply, making it tougher for locals to afford to buy. The people working low-income jobs in the service sector and/or living in neighborhoods adjacent to NoMo are being displaced as rents climb.

City planners estimate that within 20 years, Charleston's population will double, and some are worried that the character of the city that initially attracted everyone will begin to slip away.

Recovery Room
BAR

18 ⊖ MAP P50, D3

Not what it sounds like. Instead, it's a late-night dive that often swells with college students and boozy regulars in search of cheap whiskey. Various theme nights include trivia games, live music and boccie ball. (📞843-727-0999; www.recoveryroomtavern.com; 685 King St; ⌚3pm-2am Mon-Sat, noon-2am Sun)

Entertainment

Theatre 99
COMEDY

19 ⭐ MAP P50, G6

Performances and classes in improv comedy. Very funny stuff, to the point where locals drop in multiple times a week. (📞843-853-6687; www.theatre99.com; 280 Meeting St; from $5; ⌚shows 8pm Wed-Sat, sometimes 10pm)

Joseph P Riley, Jr Park
BASEBALL

20 ⭐ MAP P50, A4

Home of the RiverDogs minor league baseball team and the Citadel team. The stadium is a namesake of a long-time former Charleston mayor who regularly attends games, but it is more often referred to as 'the Joe.' On ladies night anyone wearing a skirt gets in free, and Bill Murray is a part-owner of the RiverDogs. (The Joe; 📞843-723-7241; www.riverdogs.com; 360 Fisburne St; ⌚Apr-Sep)

Shopping

Edmund's Oast Exchange
ALCOHOL

Formerly known as Charleston Beer Exchange, this beer and wine retail store (see 10 ✕ Map p50, G1) opened near its parent brewery (p54) in 2017. The two-story space has more than 1000 different varieties of booze available in cans, bottles, kegs and growlers. (📞843-990-9449; 1081 Morrison Dr; ⌚11am-8pm Tue-Sat, noon-5pm Sun)

Goat. Sheep. Cow. North.
CHEESE

21 🔒 MAP P50, G1

A gourmet cheese shop that triples as a cafe and wine bar. Get your pasteurized Spanish goat's milk and thermized Italian sheep's milk here. (📞843-203-3118; https://goatsheepcow.com; 804 Meeting St; ⌚11am-9:30pm Mon-Sat)

Explore ◈

Harleston Village, Upper King & Cannonborough Elliotborough

These three distinct neighborhoods are core areas for college students, young professionals and families to live, work, play and shop. Harleston Village is the most suburban 'hood, with stately mansions, single houses and small shops, but it's also home to the College of Charleston. Upper King is a narrow, densely packed strip of hit-or-miss restaurants, upscale boutiques and loft-style condos. Cannonborough Elliotborough attracts young creatives and families with its fixed-up Victorians and independent businesses.

Places of worship and off-beat museums and galleries abound in these neighborhoods.

Getting There & Around

These neighborhoods are all designed to be enjoyed on foot, with sidewalks and green spaces aplenty. A couple of CARTA (p151) public bus routes serve this part of the city, and Charleston's bike share program Holy Spokes (p150) also has stations around the area.

Harleston Village, Upper King & Cannonborough Elliotborough Map on p64

Walking Tour 🥾

Cannonborough Elliotborough

This unassuming, quiet neighborhood is home to much of Charleston's creative class, and the small restaurants and galleries that have sprung up to serve them are some of the city's best-kept secrets. The gentrification under way here, while unfortunate for low-income residents, has its perks for wanderers, including some lovely Charleston single houses oriented sideways with dreamy, slanted piazzas.

Walk Facts

Start Karpeles Manuscript Library Museum

End Sugar Bakeshop

Duration Two hours

❶ Karpeles Manuscript Library Museum

Exhibits at the **Karpeles Manuscript Library Museum** (p66) include Einstein's Theory of Relativity and Freud's manuscript on dreams. They rotate three times a year, which keeps the neighborhood residents stopping back in to see what's new.

❷ Elliotborough Mini Bar

Decked out in colored lights and funky art, tiny **Elliotborough Mini Bar** (📞843-577-0028; 18 Percy St; ⏱5-10pm Mon-Thu, to 11pm Fri & Sat, 3-8pm Sun) cheerfully serves beer and wine at prices locals love. The intimate venue also hosts regular live music sessions.

❸ George Gallery

The polar opposite of some of the schlocky galleries downtown, the decidedly non-touristy **George Gallery** (p66) features mostly abstract and non-objective work. The art rotates often, which keeps the regulars' interest piqued.

❹ Xiao Bao Biscuit

No matter how many times one pops into **Xiao Bao Biscuit** (p67) for a Japanese cabbage pancake, one will always be back for more. There's just nothing like a great craft cocktail with some spicy pan-Asian fare.

❺ Fuel

Round things out with a delicious mojito on the porch at **Fuel** (📞843-737-5959; www.fuelcharleston.com; 211 Rutledge Ave; ⏱11am-11pm), a classic Caribbean-themed neighborhood bar that attracts a cross section of students and young professionals.

❻ Sugar Bakeshop

The icing on the cupcake is **Sugar Bakeshop** (www.sugarbake.com; 59 1/2 Cannon St; cupcakes $3.25; ⏱10am-6pm Mon-Fri, 11am-5pm Sat), where in-the-know Charlestonians satisfy their sweet teeth, particularly on Thursday. That's Lady Baltimore day, and everybody loves this retro Southern specialty with dried fruit and white frosting.

Harleston, Upper King & Cannonborough Elliotborough

1

2

3

4

E Bay St

Drake St

Alexander St

Chapel St

Charlotte St

Elizabeth St

MAZYCK-
WRAGGBOROUGH

Calhoun St

ANSONBOROUGH

Judith St

Wragg Mall

Meeting St

John St

Marion
1 Square

For reviews see

	Sights	p66
	Eating	p67
	Drinking	p71
	Entertainment	p74
	Shopping	p74

Hampstead
Mall
Playground

EASTSIDE

America St

Amherst St

Reid St

South St

Nassau St

Mary St

Ann St

Hutson St

30

32 27

14

Hanover St

Nassau St

Columbus St

King St

Reid St

Woolfe St

Spring St

King St

28

Holly
8
Spokes

21

26

RADCLIFFBOROUGH

Vanderhorst St

Meeting St

Nassau St

25

22

12

20

11

23

St Phillip St

Coming St

Morris St

Warren St

Radcliffe St

Thomas St

19

King St

Affordabike

18

Karpeles
4 Manuscript
Library Museum

CANNONBOROUGH
ELLIOTBOROUGH

Cannon St

34

29

Percy St

Ashe St

Rose La

Bogard St

George 5
Gallery

6

Rutledge Ave

Ashley Ave

Bee St

Sumter St

Coming St

Fishburne St

Tracy St

Septima Clark Pkwy

Mitchell
Playground

WESTSIDE

Kennedy St

Line St

17

Spring St

President St

Cannon St

Race St

Perry St

Rutledge Ave

Ashley Ave

N

500 m
0.25 miles

A **B** **C** **D** **E** **F**

1

2

3

4

Harleston, Upper King & Cannonborough Elliotborough

5

Anson St
George St
Society St
Meeting St
King St **31** 🚇 ✕**15**
College of **3** Charleston 🚇
George St
St Philip St **7** ✕
Glebe St
Coming St

Calhoun St

Pitt St
Vanderhorst St
Smith St

6

Hasell St
Kahal Kadosh Beth Elohim
HISTORIC 🏛**33** DISTRICT
Market St ✕**13**
Beaufain St
West St
Wentworth St

● Urban Nirvana ✕**10**

HARLESTON VILLAGE

Bull St
Smith St
Rutledge Ave
Ashley Ave
Canon Park
Halsey St
Gadsden St
Montague St
Wentworth St

Ashley Ave
University Hospital
Mill St
Jonathan Lucas St
Calhoun St
Barre St
Halsey Blvd
President St
Courtenay Dr
Alberta Sonttle Long Lake

5
6
7

Charleston City Marina
✕**16**
Lockwood Dr

7

Horlbeck Al
Meeting St
Gibbes **2** ◉ Museum ✕**9** of Art ✕ **17**
🚇 **24** King St
Broad St
Princess St
Fulton St
Clifford St
Archdale St
Gateway Walk
Queen St
Magazine St
Logan St
Franklin St
Cromwell Al
Trapman St
Trumbo St
Colonial Lake Park
Colonial Lake
Beaufain St
Lockwood Dr
Broad St

Orange St
Legare St
New St
Short St

Ashley River

F
E
D
C
B
A

8

Sights

Marion Square
SQUARE

1 ⊙ MAP P64, E4

Charleston's most frequented park is 10 acres of green space in the middle of downtown, bordering on King, Calhoun, Meeting and Tobacco Sts. It's the home of the wildly popular Farmers Market (p74) and also houses several monuments, including a soaring statue of former Vice President John C Calhoun. (☏843-724-7327; www.nps.gov/nr/travel/charleston/mar.htm; 329 Meeting St; ⏱24hr)

Gibbes Museum of Art
GALLERY

2 ⊙ MAP P64, F7

Houses a decent collection of American and Southern works. The contemporary collection includes works by local artists, with Lowcountry life as a highlight. A 2016 renovation added a new museum store and cafe as well as 30% more gallery space. (☏843-722-2706; www.gibbesmuseum.org; 135 Meeting St; adult/child $15/6; ⏱10am-5pm Tue & Thu-Sat, to 8pm Wed, 1-5pm Sun)

College of Charleston
COLLEGE

3 ⊙ MAP P64, E5

Spread over a few city blocks at the center of Charleston's downtown, this university was founded in 1770 and is the oldest in the state. The campus is notable for its lush landscaping, which includes live oaks draped in Spanish moss, as well as its historic mansions and homes, some of which contain residence halls and Greek institutions. (☏843-805-5507; www.cofc.edu; 66 George St)

Karpeles Manuscript Library Museum
MUSEUM

4 ⊙ MAP P64, C3

An outpost of the world's largest private collection of important original manuscripts and documents, housed in a former Methodist church built in 1856. Exhibits rotate three times a year, making this a popular stop with locals. They include Einstein's Theory of Relativity, Freud's manuscript on dreams and Darwin's conclusion to his Theory of Evolution. (☏843-853-4651; https://karpeles.com/museums/cha.php; 68 Spring St; admission free; ⏱11am-4pm Tue-Sun)

George Gallery
ART STUDIO

5 ⊙ MAP P64, B2

A neighborhood favorite, this contemporary art gallery displays mostly abstract and non-objective work of artists from the East Coast with some connection to Charleston. There are no actual rules, though – just whatever the owner feels like. (☏843-579-7328; http://georgegalleryart.com; 50 Bogard St; ⏱10am-5pm Tue-Fri, 11am-5pm Sat)

Eating

Xiao Bao Biscuit ASIAN $

6 MAP P64, B3

Housed in a former gas station, with exposed-brick walls and concrete floor – this casual but stylish eatery hits the hipster high marks. But the food? Now we're talking. The short but palate-kicking menu spotlights simple pan-Asian fare enhanced by local ingredients and spicy flavors. For something different and memorable, try the *okonomiyaki* – a Japanese cabbage pancake – with egg and bacon. (www.xiaobaobiscuit.com; 224 Rutledge Ave; lunch mains $12, dinner mains $12-16; 11:30am-2pm & 5:30-10pm Mon-Sat)

Basic Kitchen HEALTH FOOD $$

7 MAP P64, E6

With dishes like avo toast, fresh sesame kale and rainbow bowls (which come with sweet-potato noodles, veggies, herbs and Thai peanut sauce), this healthy and delicious little cafe feels like something you'd stumble across in Bali. The surfboard decor and yummy fresh fruit juices do nothing to dispel that impression; and clearly, vegetarians are well served here. (843-789-4568; https://basickitchen.com; 82 Wentworth St; breakfast & lunch mains $8-14, dinner mains $13-23; 8-10:30am, 11am-3pm & 5:30-9pm Mon-Fri, 9am-3pm & 5:30-9pm Sat, 9am-3pm Sun;)

Marion Square

GORDON BELL/SHUTTERSTOCK ©

Gateway Walk

A loose, natural-feeling path, the **Gateway Walk** (Map p64) winds through several church grounds and over-grown graveyards between St John's Lutheran Church and St Philip's Church. The walk is particularly lovely during spring, when the wildflowers are in bloom.

Juanita Greenberg's Nacho Royale

MEXICAN $

8 🍴 MAP P64, D4

Nachos are front and center at this tasty, affordable Mexican joint on King St, and locals go wild for it with good reason. The nacho royales arrive Mexican-pizza-style, with corn or flour chips and your choice of veggies, beans, steak, tofu, shrimp, pulled chicken and basically anything else you can dream of. Boring people can also get burritos or tacos. (🕿843-723-6224; https://juanitagreenbergs.com; 439 King St; nachos $9-11; ⏱11am-2am)

Poogan's Porch

SOUTHERN US $$

9 🍴 MAP P64, F7

It's very Charlestonian to take brunch on the terrace of this cozy but elegant two-story Victorian, where the homemade buttermilk biscuits are out of control and the chicken and waffles are second

to none. Boozy brunchers have their pick of mimosas, cocktails, craft beer and 1500 bottles of wine in the cellar. (🕿843-577-2337; www.poogansporch.com; 72 Queen St; brunch mains $10-14, dinner mains $21-34; ⏱10:30am-2:30pm & 5-9:30pm Mon-Fri, 9am-2:30pm & 5-9:30pm Sat & Sun)

Circa 1886

SOUTHERN US $$$

10 🍴 MAP P64, D7

In a renovated, elegant carriage house, this is Lowcountry fine dining at its most rewarding, with healthful, seasonal offerings that reflect the region's bounty and build on its traditions. Adventurous diners will appreciate the coffee-brined antelope, which comes with sorghum sweet-potato mousseline and shishito peppers. Everybody will lose it for the benne-crusted (sesame-crusted) duck breast with white peach grits.

There's also an extensive wine list, and the waitstaff are highly knowledgeable and gracious. (🕿843-853-7828; www.circa1886.com; 149 Wentworth St; mains $34-40, tasting menu $90; ⏱5:30-10pm Mon-Sat)

Darling Oyster Bar

SEAFOOD $$

11 🍴 MAP P64, D3

Not all oysters are created equal in Charleston, but the Darling serves up the raw goodness. Its light, flavorful selections originate in places like Prince Edward Island and arrive at the table with a mild ginger mignonette. The Creole shrimp channels N'awlins and kills it, the lightly cured ceviche is highly refreshing, and the cocktails are crafty and delicious. (📞843-641-0821; http://thedarling.com; 513 King St; mains $10-27; ⏱4pm-late)

Ordinary   SEAFOOD $$

12 MAP P64, D2

Inside a cavernous 1927 bank building, this buzzy seafood hall and oyster bar feels like the best party in town. The menu is short, but the savory dishes are prepared with finesse – from the oyster sliders to the lobster rolls to the nightly fish dishes. (📞843-414-7060; www.eattheordinary.com; 544 King St; dishes $10-33; ⏱5-10:30pm Tue-Sun)

Le Farfalle   TUSCAN $$$

13 MAP P64, E6

Seafood charcuterie doesn't get better than the octopus carpaccio at Le Farfalle, a breath of fresh Tuscan air with a spacious, bright dining room and cheeky yet sophisticated waitstaff. The warm rosemary focaccia, housemade pastas and mains (ie roasted duck and sea bass) are all dreams on plates, and the extensive wine list makes for delightful pairings. (📞843-212-0920; http://lefarfalle charleston.com; 15 Beaufain St; pasta $17-26, mains $28-42; ⏱11:30am-2:30pm & 5:30-11pm Mon-Sat, 10:30am-2:30pm & 5:30-11pm Sun)

Halls Chophouse   STEAK $$$

14 MAP P64, D4

Hands down the best restaurant for getting all done up, squeezing in at the bar and ordering a sizable, rare cut of steak with several glasses of Napa Valley cabernet. (📞843-727-0090; https://hallschop house.com; 434 King St; steaks from $40; ⏱5-11pm Sun-Thu, to midnight Fri & Sat)

Leyla Fine Lebanese Cuisine   LEBANESE $$$

15 MAP P64, E5

A welcome respite from all the Lowcountry and fried food, this elegant Lebanese restaurant is a favorite with locals. You can't really go wrong, so you might as well do it all with a sampler of hummus,

Spa Day

On the grounds of the Wentworth Mansion, in gorgeously converted former stables, the elegant, relaxing **Urban Nirvana** (Map p64; 📞843-724-6555; www.urbannirvana.com; 141 Wentworth St; ⏱9am-7pm Mon-Sat, 11am-6pm Sun) spa is defined by brick and exposed wood beams. Complete with heated blankets and aromatic oils, the treatments are nothing short of transportive. The woman who does the facials (from $60) is a real pro.

tabouleh, baba ganoush, falafel, fried kibbe and lots of other goodness. There are plenty of good vegetarian options. (☎843-501-7500; http://leyla-charleston.com; 298 King St; mains $24-38; ⏰11:30am-9pm Tue-Thu & Sun, to 10pm Fri & Sat; 🥗)

Marina Variety Store

SOUTHERN US $

16 🍴 MAP P64, A7

A long-standing, down-home, greasy-spoon kinda place, with harbor views and Southern hospitality as warm as the buttermilk biscuits. Thumbs up to the grits, fried green tomatoes and crab cake Benedict. Put the gravy on everything. (☎843-723-6325; www.varietystorerestaurant.com; 17 Lockwood Dr; mains from $6; ⏰6:30am-4pm & 5-9pm Mon-Sat, 6:30am-3pm Sun)

Husk

SOUTHERN US $$$

17 🍴 MAP P64, F7

The creation of acclaimed chef Sean Brock, Husk is one of the South's most buzzed-about restaurants, which can be a disadvantage. How can the food possibly compete with the hype? (The fried chicken skins definitely don't.) Every ingredient is grown or raised in the South and the offerings change daily. The setting, in a two-story mansion, is elegant but unfussy. (☎843-577-2500; www.huskrestaurant.com; 76 Queen St; brunch & lunch $10-17, dinner $29-34; ⏰11:30am-2:30pm Mon-Sat, 5:30-10pm Sun-Thu, 5:30-11pm Fri & Sat, brunch 10am-2:30pm Sun)

Husk

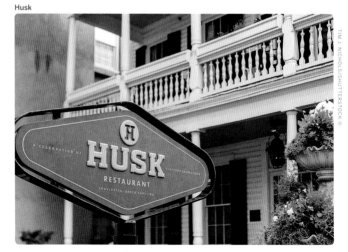

TIM J. NICHOLS/SHUTTERSTOCK ©

Grocery

AMERICAN $$$

18 ❌ MAP P64, C3

Set in an industrial-chic space adorned with mason jars of pickled everything, this is Charleston's farm-to-table champion, with a fiercely locavore and vegetarian-friendly approach, and cooking styles channeling both the South and the Mediterranean. Seasonal ingredients arrive fresh from nearby farmers, foragers and fishermen, and chef/owner Kevin Johnson combines them in innovative and deeply satisfying ways. (☎843-302-8825; www. thegrocerycharleston.com; 4 Cannon St; mains $28-30; ⏱5-10pm Tue-Sat, 10am-2:30pm & 5-10pm Sun; 🍴)

Drinking

High Wire Distilling

DISTILLERY

19 🍺 MAP P64, C1

A bright downtown tasting room where you take shots of small-batch gin, whiskey, vodka and amaro, right in a row. Tasty cocktails are also available, and the 'bee's knees' (with botanical gin, lemon, honey and lavender) is a doozy.

Tours of the distillery run Tuesday through Saturday every hour (on the hour) from 11am to 6pm. Make a reservation. (☎843-755-4664; http://highwiredistilling.squarespace. com; 652 King St; ⏱9am-6pm Tue-Fri, 11am-6pm Sat)

Culinary Conundrums 🍽

So little time, so much deliciousness. Narrowing down where to eat on Upper King is the great Charleston challenge. The varied and eclectic eateries of Cannonborough Elliotborough don't make things easier.

Prohibition

COCKTAIL BAR

20 🍺 MAP P64, D3

This delightful Jazz Age gastropub serves up excellent craft cocktails (from $10) that tend to pair well with the lip-smackin' Southern grub. Think a 'bacon maple old-fashioned' cocktail with some deviled eggs, or a mint julep with shrimp and grits. There's also a sweet dance floor, and free swing-dancing lessons are offered Wednesday and Sunday at 6:30pm. It's a total hoot. (☎843-793-2964; https://prohibitioncharleston.com; 547 King St; ⏱5pm-1am Mon-Thu, 5pm-2am Fri, 11am-2am Sat, 11am-1am Sun)

Proof

COCKTAIL BAR

21 🍺 MAP P64, D4

It may be snug in here, but the cocktails ($9 to $13) sure are first-class and their mixologist is some kind of visionary. Case in point: the 'knuckleball' has Old Grand-Dad, a spicy cola reduction, orange bitters and pickled boiled

peanuts. (📞843-793-1422; www.
charlestonproof.com; 437 King
St; 🕐4pm-2am Mon-Fri, 6pm-2am
Sat & Sun)

Pour Taproom

CRAFT BEER

22 📍 MAP P64, D2

A brewpub with a cool concept:
on-tap, self-serve craft beer, wine
and cocktails, where you pour it
yourself and pay by the ounce. It's
downtown, on the 9th floor of the
Historic District Hyatt. There are
also appetizers and sandwiches.
(📞843-779-0810; www.charleston.
pourtaproom.com; 560 King St; 🕐4-
11pm Mon-Thu, noon-1am Fri & Sat,
noon-11pm Sun)

St Michael's Episcopal Church

MEUNIERD/SHUTTERSTOCK ©

Charleston Distilling Co

DISTILLERY

23 📍 MAP P64, D3

A farm-to-bottle, independently
owned, small-batch distillery on
King St. Grab a flight of spirits or a
cocktail and take a tour ($5) of the
distillery, a sleek space with inlaid
brick and wood paneling. Do it fast,
though. Word on the street is that
the business may move to John's
Island to expand their operations.
(📞843-718-1446; www.charleston
distilling.com; 501 King St; 🕐11am-
7pm, closed Wed & Sun)

Bar at Husk

BAR

Adjacent to the restaurant Husk
(see 18 🍴 Map p64, F7), this intimate
brick-and-worn-wood spot recalls
a speakeasy, with classic cocktails
($10 to $15), sphere ice and
passionate attention to detail.
(📞843-577-2500; www.husk
restaurant.com/about/bar; 76 Queen
St; 🕐4pm-late)

Bin 152

WINE BAR

24 📍 MAP P64, F7

From the same couple behind
Chez Nous comes this elegant
downtown wine bar (glasses from
$15). It's low-lit, chic and fes-
tooned in impressive, rotating art
and antiques (all for sale). But the
best reason to go is to pair the adventurous wine selections with imported cheese (from $10), freshly
baked bread and other charcuterie
bits. (📞843-577-7359; www.bin152.
com; 152 King St; 🕐4pm-2am)

Understanding Religion

The New World was mostly populated by colonies founded by certain religious sects. Charleston was not among them. The 'Holy City,' as it came to be known for its multitudes of churches, was instead a haven for religious tolerance, and today more than 400 houses of worship call Charleston home.

The Most Famous Churches

Part of being the 'Holy City' is that your skyline should be defined by its steeples and spires. That's why in Charleston the law dictates that no building can be higher than the tallest church steeple.

The oldest church in Charleston (that's still standing) is St Michael's Episcopal Church, which dates back to 1761 and has seen the likes of George Washington and Robert E Lee worship here. Its bells are a big deal, and have been announcing the time and various events, including earthquakes, hurricanes, fires and attacks on the city, for more than 250 years.

The second most prominent church, St Philip's, was erected in 1835, but its Anglican congregation is older than that of St Michael's. Many famous people are buried in the church cemetery, one end point of the Gateway Walk (p68) through several church grounds.

The French Huguenots

Some of the earliest religious refugees to take Charleston up on its invitation were the French Huguenots, who were part of a Protestant movement that was largely rejected in France. The English, however, were happy to receive the Huguenots, particularly because many of them were prosperous merchants and professionals.

Jewish Heritage

In the heart of Charleston, **Kahal Kadosh Beth Elohim** (Map p64; ☎843-723-1090; www.kkbe.org; 90 Hasell St; ☺10am-4pm Sun-Fri) is the oldest continuously used synagogue in the country, and the birthplace of the American Reform Judaism movement.

Alley

BOWLING

25 🜨 MAP P64, D2

Super-fun bar to play Skee-Ball, table hockey, bowling and Pop-A-Shot. They've also got arcade games and decent pub food. Wednesday is trivia night and Tuesday has $2 bowling lanes after 9pm. (☎843-818-4080; www.thealleycharleston.com; 131 Columbus St; per lane per hour Sun-Thu $35, Fri &

Sat $45; ◷4pm-2am Mon-Wed, 11am-2am Thu-Sun)

Kudu
COFFEE, CRAFT BEER

26 🟢 MAP P64, D4

Rock up at 6:45am and order an excellent espresso or craft booze – we're not judging – at this hipster cafe and beer bar located just off Marion Sq.

Beer-wise there are a total of 20 taps, including a featured cask-conditioned ale, while the coffee menu and execution would make any barista proud. Take either in the courtyard, complete with gurgling fountain. (www.kuducoffeeandcraftbeer.com; 4 Vanderhorst St; ◷6:45am-9pm Mon-Fri, 7am-9pm Sat, 8am-8pm Sun)

Entertainment

Charleston Music Hall
LIVE PERFORMANCE

27 ⭐ MAP P64, E4

An intimate performance venue with great acoustics and not a bad seat in the house. Ideal for live music or theater. (☎843-853-2252; www.charlestonmusichall.com; 37 John St; ◷box office 10am-3pm Mon-Fri)

Music Farm
CONCERT VENUE

28 ⭐ MAP P64, D3

A popular downtown concert venue, with local and national acts

from every imaginable genre. The place isn't very big; in the summertime it often fills up and gets pretty sweaty. (☎843-577-6989; http://musicfarm.com; 32 Ann St; ◷varies)

Shopping

Beads on Cannon
JEWELRY

29 🔒 MAP P64, B3

A massive store, with two floors full of stones, Czech glass, wire, leather, chains, Swarovski crystal, tools and rhinestones. The store also offers jewelry-making classes. (☎843-723-5648; www.beadsoncannon.com; 87 Cannon St; ◷11am-5pm)

Farmers Market
MARKET

30 🔒 MAP P64, E4

Stop by this terrific farmers market on Saturdays for local produce, homemade food and drinks, art, music, boiled peanuts and more. (www.charlestonfarmersmarket.com; Marion Sq; ◷8am-2pm Sat Apr-Nov)

Croghan's Jewel Box
JEWELRY

31 🔒 MAP P64, E5

Long-standing, family-owned jewelry store, offering pricey but gorgeous antique pieces, estate finds, engagement rings and other one-of-a-kind gifts on Upper King. (☎843-723-3594; www.croghans jewelbox.com; 308 King St; ◷10am-5:30pm Mon-Fri, to 5pm Sat)

Blue Bicycle Books
BOOKS

32 🔒 MAP P64, E4

Excellent new-and-used store with a great selection on Southern history and culture. (📞843-722-2666; www.bluebicyclebooks.com; 420 King St; 🕙10am-7:30pm Mon-Sat, 1-6pm Sun)

Charleston Crafts Cooperative
ARTS & CRAFTS

33 🔒 MAP P64, F6

A pricey, well-edited selection of contemporary South Carolina–made crafts, such as sweetgrass baskets, hand-dyed silks and wood carvings. (📞843-723-2938; www.charlestoncrafts.org; 161 Church St; 🕙10am-6pm)

Indigo & Cotton
CLOTHING

34 🔒 MAP P64, B3

Stocks high-end and innovative brands of clothing, footwear and accessories: for instance, Raleigh

Farmers Market

JEREMEY LENDE/SHUTTERSTOCK ©

Denim, a company that stitches its jeans on vintage sewing machines. (📞843-718-2980; https://indigoandcotton.com; 79 Cannon St; 🕙11am-6pm Mon-Fri, to 5pm Sat)

Explore ⊚
Charleston County Sea Islands

A dozen islands within an hour's drive of Charleston make up the Charleston County Sea Islands. Around 10 miles southeast of Charleston on the Mt Pleasant side, Sullivan's Island and Isle of Palms beckon day-trippers for sand-lounging and reveling on blue-sky days. Around 4 miles in the other direction brings you to James Island, one of the most urban of Charleston's barrier sea islands. Further south, Folly Beach is good for a day of sun and sand. The other end of the island is popular with surfers.

Upscale rental homes, golf courses and the swanky Sanctuary resort mark Kiawah Island, southwest of Charleston, where you'll find lucky visitors cruising on their bikes along one of the most gorgeous beaches in the South. Nearby Edisto Island (ed-is-tow) is a home-spun family vacation spot without a single traffic light.

Getting There & Around

Charleston's barrier sea islands are all accessed via a series of byways and bridges from the city, though not always with a connection from one to another. You'll need to take the long way round if you want to go from Sullivan's Island to Kiawah or Edisto Islands, for example.

Charleston County Sea Islands Map on p82

Folly Beach (p84) AARON HYSLOP/SHUTTERSTOCK ©

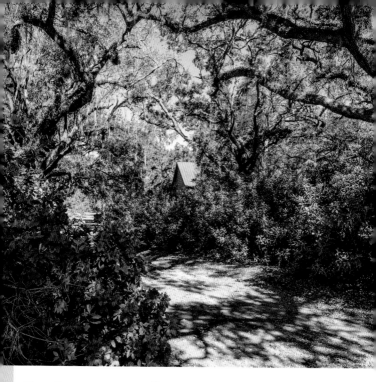

Top Experience 📷

Understand the Story of the South at McLeod Plantation

Many of the plantations around Charleston once belonged to the city's very wealthiest denizens. McLeod is not among them. The upper-middle-class owners of this Sea Island cotton farm strived to keep pace, and the enslaved workers were pushed to their limits. This sight is among the best for understanding of the prolonged mistreatment of African Americans in the South.

◉ MAP P82, E3

📞 843-795-4386

www.ccprc.com/1447/McLeod-Plantation-Historic-Site

325 Country Club Dr, James Island

adult/child $15/6

🕙 9am-4pm Tue-Sun

McLeod Home

This 19th-century Victorian-style plantation home isn't furnished or particularly grand. The ground floor contains what was once a formal parlor, a dining room and a small library with simple woodwork. A 1920s renovation reversed the orientation and the backdoor became the front entrance and a small porch was replaced by a new portico with columns. An indoor kitchen was also installed.

While the house isn't much to see, the story of its unique series of occupants is revelatory. They include the McLeod family, the Confederate army, the Union army, a federal agency that aimed to help ex-slaves transition to freedom, and the Charleston County Park & Recreation Commission.

Transition Row

A row of cramped, basic wooden cabins on the property was originally built to house slaves, and until 1960 the cabins offered no electricity or running water (only one house ever included indoor plumbing). After the war, the cabins became transitional housing for freed slaves, and a look inside gives visitors considerable insight into how generations of Gullah families lived.

After the McLeods regained control of the property, the cabins were rented out as family homes, often to the descendants of former slaves, until the last McLeod's death in 1990.

Places of Worship

Over the years, there were a couple of different structures that served as places of worship on the McLeod Plantation. In one of the old barns, a minister who was paid by Mr McLeod preached to African Americans about how they were to serve God by obediently performing their duties on the plantation.

The property also contains a former slave cabin that was converted into a worship house

★ **Top Tips**

○ Bring tissues; even the tour guides here occasionally break down crying.

○ Researcher Barbara Brundage occasionally gives highly informative and engaging tours; call ahead and time your visit for when she's working.

○ Enrich your experience by downloading the Transition to Freedom app from Apple's App store, or borrow an Apple device from the welcome center.

○ Arrive a bit before the formal tour to wander the grounds and read displays; you'll get more out of the guided tour.

Occupants of the McLeod Plantation

The McLeod plantation home was built by slave labor just before the Civil War, and its first owner, William Wallace McLeod, also ordered a fence constructed around the house, which he referred to as 'the enclosure.' This was to separate his family space from the homes of the enslaved.

During the Civil War, the McLeod family (and all island residents) were forced to evacuate, and the plantation was occupied by Confederate soldiers. In 1865 the Union army took control of the island and made the McLeod plantation their headquarters, then turned it over to the Bureau for Refugees, Freedmen and Abandoned Lands, a government agency that helped transition four million ex-slaves to freedom. The home briefly served as a school for freed children and as a medical treatment facility, and parcels of the land were doled out to ex-slaves to build new lives.

In 1868 the political climate changed, the agency helping ex-slaves shuttered its doors and the McLeod family managed to claw back the property. For the next 100 years, the family maintained control over a work force of ex-slaves that lived and toiled in much the same conditions as they had before the war. Laws were passed that resembled the old slave code, punishments continued to be more severe than in a free-labor society, and the dream of land ownership receded into impossibility as payment for labor came in food rations and a portion of the harvest.

The last member of the McLeod family died in 1990 and left instructions in a will for the plantation to be preserved. Today it is managed by the Charleston County Park & Recreation Commission.

in the 1970s. From here, the Children of God Mission regaled James Island residents with gospel music via transistor radio.

Gullah Cemetery

Perhaps the most telling site on the plantation grounds is a wooded area that doubles as a Gullah cemetery, where more than 100 people are anonymously buried. The remains of children are contained in 42 of the graves, a testament to the brutal conditions on the plantation. Gullah people believed in an afterlife in which they rejoined their African ancestors.

Charleston County Sea Islands

A　　B　　C　　D

1

Delamare Hwy

165

Ashley River Rd

Charleston International ✈ Airport

2

County Line Rd

Hyde Park Rd

Davison Rd

Bees Ferry Rd

17 **Savannah Hwy**

Savannah Hwy　● Rantowles

3

New Rd

17

165

Salters Hill Rd

Chisholm Rd

Main Rd

Maybank Hwy
✕✕
9 14

Hollywood ●

162

● Meggett

Johns Island ●

◎ *Angel*
1 *Oak Tree*

Johns Island

4

Bears Bluff Rd

700

Wadmalaw Island

Bohicket Rd

River Rd

5

◎✕ 13
16

Charleston 2
Tea Plantation ◎

Maybank Hwy

Betsy Kerrison Pkwy

Kiawah Island ●

Governors Dr

✕ 10

● Rockville

Seabrook Island

Kiawah
3 Beachwater Park

6

174

Edisto Island Serpentarium

◎ 6

◎ 5 *Botany Bay Plantation Wildlife Management Area*

Seabrook Island ●

Devereaux Bank

A　　B　　C　　D

Charleston County Sea Islands

E | F | G | H

1

2

3

4

5

6

Hanahan

Rivers Ave

Amtrak

North Charleston

Greyhound

North Charleston Visitor Center

Mark Clark Expwy

526

526

41

17

Eagle Island

Goat Island

Isle of Palms

517

703

Rifle Range Rd

Drum Island

Mount Pleasant

Patriots Point

Saint Andrews

McLeod Plantation

Charleston

30

Sullivans Island

Fort Moultrie

Isle of Palms 18

Sullivan's Island 12

8

700

17

James Island County Park

Centerville

Fort Johnson Rd

Morris Island

Charleston Executive Airport

James Island

Folly Rd

Goat Island

Folly Island

Long Island

11

7

15

Folly Beach

4

Folly Beach County Park

Kiawah Island

ATLANTIC OCEAN

0 — 10 km
0 — 5 miles

For reviews see

◉	Top Experiences	p78
⊙	Sights	p84
✕	Eating	p86
🍷	Drinking	p88
✪	Entertainment	p89

Sights

Angel Oak Tree HISTORIC SITE

1 ◎ MAP P82, D4

Some folks reckon this Southern live oak tree is 1500 years old (others says it's 400 to 500 years old). Whatever the case, it's one of the oldest living organisms east of the Mississippi, standing 66.5ft tall and measuring 28ft around. Its thick branches shoot off in all directions, in many cases twisting to the ground and back up again. There's no climbing allowed.

A small gift shop contains tree art and various books, and about 15 signs forbidding visitors from reading the books without purchasing them. (☎843-559-3496; www.angel oaktree.com; 3688 Angel Oak Rd, Johns Island; admission free; ◎9am-5pm Mon-Sat, 1-5pm Sun, gift shop till 4:30)

Charleston Tea Plantation PLANTATION

2 ◎ MAP P82, B5

There's only one large-scale, working tea plantation in the US,

folks, and this is it. A trolley tour takes visitors around the property, offering plenty of information on its history, while a free tour of the production facility gives insight into the magic behind green, oolong and black tea. The gift shop has lots of goodies and souvenirs, including free, bottomless hot and cold tea. (☎843-559-0383; www. charlestonteaplantation.com; 6617 Maybank Hwy, Wadmalaw Island; trolley tour adult/child under 13yr $12/6; ◎10am-4pm Mon-Sat, noon-4pm Sun)

Kiawah Beachwater Park BEACH

3 ◎ MAP P82, C6

This idyllic stretch of sun-toasted sand at the southern end of Kiawah Island has been called one of the top 10 beaches in the USA and is the only publicly accessible beach on Kiawah. Take a bike – the compact sand is perfect for a ride along the 10-mile barrier island. (www.ccprc.com; 8 Beachwalker Dr, Kiawah Island; parking $5; ◎9am-8pm May-Sep, shorter hours rest of year)

Folly Beach County Park PARK

4 ◎ MAP P82, E5

At the far west end of Folly Beach, this scenic county park features a serene swimming beach and a pelican rookery. Public changing areas and beach-chair rentals are available. Lifeguards are on duty seasonally. (☎843-762-9960; www. ccprc.com; 1100 W Ashley Ave, Folly Island; parking $5-15; ◎9am-8pm May-Aug, shorter hours rest of year)

Historic fort

Fort Moultrie (☎843-883-3123; www.nps.gov/fosu; 1214 Middle St, Sullivan's Island; adult/child $3/ free; ◎9am-5pm), at the mouth of Charleston Harbor, encapsulates the history of US coastal defense spanning nearly 200 years and four wars.

Botany Bay Plantation Wildlife Management Area

WILDLIFE RESERVE

5 ◉ MAP P82, B6

An avenue of regal live oaks flanks the entrance to this 4687-acre wildlife preserve, where a mix of pine forests, agricultural fields, coastal islands and two miles of undeveloped beach await. There's a 6.5-mile wildlife drive through the forest, which features plenty of birds and fox squirrels.

And the beach, which can only be accessed on foot, offers a peek at some coastline that looks similar to how it did when the original settlers arrived. In the 1800s the area was home to two successful Sea Island cotton plantations, Bleak Hall and Sea Cloud. (☏843-442-8140; Edisto Island; admission free; ☉sunrise-sunset Wed-Sun; 👪)

Edisto Island Serpentarium

ZOO

6 ◉ MAP P82, A6

Around 50 years of reptile obsession by owners Ted and Heyward Clamp culminate in this serpentarium, which differs from most in that you can see snakes living in their natural habitats, separated from visitors by low-walled enclosures rather than glass. Alligators, lizards, turtles and crocodiles also live here. Think of it as a reptilian Disneyland. (☏843-869-1171; www.edistoserpentarium.com; 1374 Hwy 174, Edisto Island; adult/child $15/11; ☉10am-6pm Mon-Sat Jun-early Sep, hours vary Thu-Sat spring & fall)

Angel Oak Tree

Worth a Trip: Bulls Island

For a further-flung island adventure, nature enthusiasts will appreciate **Bulls Island** (📞843-881-4582; www.bullsislandferry.com; Awendaw; ferry ride $40), about an hour's drive north of Charleston. Its pristine shores can be reached via ferry (a 15-minute ride from the mainland), and captains often share their wealth of knowledge on the island's attractions, which include hiking trails, great shelling, numerous alligators and a 'boneyard' beach with spooky, bare trees poking up through the sand. It's wise to bring sunscreen, comfy shoes, a beach towel and some food. The boat stays at the island for a little over three hours, then heads back to the mainland.

If you've still got energy at this point, it's totally worth it to continue driving north to McClellanville, a quaint little fishing town with oak-lined streets and lovely Victorians. The superlative seafood joint **TW Graham & Co** (📞843-887-4342; http://twgrahamcoseafood.webs.com; 810 Pinckney St; mains $7-12; ⏱11am-2:30pm Tue-Sun & 5:30-9:30pm Thu-Sat) has expertly fried seafood and decadent key lime pie. Those who really like to make the most of their travels should consider a drive over a dirt road through the woods to the **St James Santee Parish Church** (Brick Church at Wambaw; Old Georgetown Rd, McClellanville), a little brick house of worship built in 1768 for the French Huguenots.

Another worthwhile attraction in the area is the **Center for Birds of Prey** (📞843-971-7474; www.thecenterforbirdsofprey.org; 4719 Hwy 17 N, Awendaw; tour & flight demonstration adult/child 6-12yr $18/12; ⏱10am-5pm Thu-Sat), where owls, hawks, falcons, kites, vultures and eagles are rehabilitated. Those that cannot be released stay within the 152-acre conservation area, and some birds do flying demonstrations.

Eating

Bowens Island Restaurant
SEAFOOD $

7 🍽 MAP P82, F4

Down a long dirt road through Lowcountry marshland near Folly Beach, this unpainted wooden shack is one of the South's most venerable seafood dives – grab an oyster knife and start shucking!

A half/full tray runs $12/17. Cool beer and friendly locals give the place its soul. (www.bowensisland. biz; 1870 Bowens Island Rd, Folly Island; mains $8-18; ⏱5-9:30pm Tue-Sat)

Obstinate Daughter
AMERICAN $$

8 🍽 MAP P82, G3

Sullivan's Island wasn't on the region's culinary map till this place showed up and made serious waves. The chef/owner, who also received high praise for Wild Olive, has demonstrated considerable range here, refocusing on light and playful plates of fresh veggies, pasta, seafood and unusual ingredients. Raw oysters are flown in from top locales, and vegetarians will leave exuberant.

The sun-drenched dining room is up on the 2nd floor, while a downstairs coffee shop and retail space offers strong coffee and lip-smacking gelato. (843-416-5020; www.theobstinatedaughter.com; 2063 Middle St, Sullivan's Island; pizza from $15, mains $10-27; 11am-10pm Mon-Fri, 10am-10pm Sat & Sun;)

Wild Olive ITALIAN $$

9 MAP P82, D3

This cozy Italian kitchen on Johns Island is whipping up some of the best homemade pastas and ambitious mains outside of Tuscany. The *carne crudo* is light and artful, and the lamb-sausage lasagna is a gooey delight that warmed us from the inside. Other favorites include charred octopus and ricotta gnocchi, and the homemade limoncello was a lovely touch.

The wine list is extensive and impressive. (843-737-4177; www. wildoliverestaurant.com; 2867 Maybank Hwy, Johns Island; pastas $13-22, mains $20-37; 5:30-10pm Sun-Thu, to 11:30pm Fri & Sat, bar from 4pm; P)

Jasmine Porch SOUTHERN US $$$

10 MAP P82, D5

Kiawah Island is a private island, mostly for fancy golfers and other well-off folks. But tell 'em at the gate you're headed to Jasmine Porch and, boom, you're in. The charming Southern kitchen is ensconced in the Sanctuary resort and its spacious dining room is defined by a sky-high ceiling, oak-plank flooring and elegant brick.

This is the place for she-crab soup, fried green tomatoes and anything from the sea, which you can also look out at through floor-to-ceiling windows. (843-768-6330; https://kiawahresort.com/dining/jasmine-porch; Kiawah Island; small plates $10-16, mains $26-36; 6:30-11am, 11:30am-2pm & 5:30pm-late Mon-Sat, 6:30-10:15am, 11:45am-2pm & 5:30pm-late Sun)

Jack of Cups PUB FOOD $

11 MAP P82, F4

This local watering hole looks like your average neighborhood pub, with a sunny back patio, to boot. But the from-scratch menu, which

Freeze your bills off

The **Bill Murray Look-a-Like Polar Plunge** (Folly Beach) is a sub-zero swim that pays homage to Charleston's most distinguished resident each New Year's Day. Participants attempting to resemble Bill Murray in various roles, and everyone is encouraged to 'freeze your bills off.' Prizes are given to the best costumes.

changes daily, really sets it apart. The curries are excellent, and the mulligatawny soup – a red lentil concoction with Indian spices and apple puree on top – is rightfully famous. (☏843-633-0042; www.jackofcups.com; 34 Center St, Folly Beach; mains $9-12; ⏰kitchen noon-10pm Wed-Mon, bar open later)

Poe's Tavern   PUB FOOD $

12 🚇 MAP P82, G3

On a sunny day the front porch of Poe's on Sullivan's Island is the place to be. The tavern's namesake, master of the macabre Edgar Allan Poe, was once stationed at nearby Fort Moultrie. The burgers are good, and the Amontillado comes with guacamole, jalapeño jack, pico de gallo and chipotle sour cream. Quoth the raven: 'Gimme more.' (☏843-883-0083; www.poestavern.com; 2210 Middle St, Sullivan's Island; mains $9-13; ⏰11am-midnight)

Drinking

Firefly Distillery   DISTILLERY

13 🚇 MAP P82, B5

The world's first hand-crafted sweet-tea-flavored vodka came from this gem of a distillery, tucked into the forest on Wadmalaw Island. Sampling this classic, which is made with tea grown on the nearby Charleston Tea Plantation (p84), distilled four times and blended with sugarcane from Louisiana, is what brings most people to the door. Tastings are $6.

Once inside, though, guests sample a great many other libations, including flavored moonshines (the peach is insanely delicious), liqueurs that taste just like pies, and craft beer. Next door, Deep Water Vineyard, the only vineyard in the region, offers tastings as well, and on Saturdays there's also live music and food trucks. (☏843-557-1405; http://fireflyspirits.com; 6775 Bears Bluff Rd, Wadmalaw Island; ⏰11am-5pm Tue-Sat)

Low Tide Brewing   BREWERY

14 🚇 MAP P82, D3

A friendly neighborhood brewery with 12 taps spouting solid craft beers, including stouts, sours, ales and lagers. We like the Romance in the Dark, a dark sour with a hint of cherry flavor. A flight of four costs $7. (☏843-501-7570; http://lowtidebrewing.com; 2836 Maybank Hwy, Johns Island; ⏰3-10pm Mon-Thu, noon-midnight Fri & Sat, noon-10pm Sun)

Chico Feo   PUB

15 🚇 MAP P82, F4

A laid-back local favorite serving beer and wine, and also a range of tasty international dishes, from acai bowls to tacos to burritos to *bun cha* (a Vietnamese stew). (☏843-906-2710; www.chicofeos.com; 122 E Ashley Ave, Folly Beach; ⏰noon-2am Mon-Thu, 11am-2am Fri-Sun)

Deep Water Vineyard   WINERY

16 🕐 MAP P82, B5

OK, so muscadine wine isn't usually at the top of an oenophile's list. It is, however, a fine product of South Carolina, and at this here winery (the only one in the Charleston area, mind you), a few of them aren't that terrible. The owners bring in some grapes from California to make interesting blends with their own. Tastings are $7.

So although most of the wines still have that syrupy muscadine flavor, some kinda don't.Next door is Firefly Distillery, where the moonshine and liquors go down smooth as pie. (📞843-559-6867; www.deepwatervineyard.com; 6775 Bears Bluff Rd, Wadmalaw Island; 🕐10am-5pm Tue-Sat)

Entertainment

Pour House   CONCERT VENUE

17 ⭐ MAP P82, E3

An intimate local music venue, with a very chill back patio. College kids and twenty-somethings dig it.

Nightlife

Folly Beach is the best (and edgiest) for nightlife, with a few bars in the island's center by the Tides Hotel. Sullivan's Island skews yuppie and has great people-watching. Isle of Palms has a good scene as well, particularly in the summer. There are a few good craft breweries on Johns Island.

(📞843-571-4343; http://charleston pourhouse.com; 1977 Maybank Hwy, James Island; concerts from $12; 🕐4pm-2am Mon-Fri, to midnight Sat, 11am-2am Sun)

Windjammer   LIVE MUSIC

18 ⭐ MAP P82, H3

A long-standing beach bar with good live music Thursday through Saturday nights. Occasional karaoke, too. (📞843-886-8596; www. the-windjammer.com/wp; 1008 Ocean Blvd, Isle of Palms; tickets from $5; 🕐11am-1:30am)

Worth a Trip 🔭
Explore Fort Sumter National Monument

Fort Sumter National Monument, where the first shots of the Civil War were fired, certainly draws the crowds. Across the harbor on Sullivan's Island, Fort Moultrie and its richly layered history are also part of the monument. Together these fortifications illuminate the power struggles that plagued Charleston Harbor through four major wars and over 200 years.

Getting There

Take the **Fort Sumter Boat Tour** (Map p50, H4; www.fortsumtertours. com; adult/child 4-11yr $22/14) from Liberty Sq and Patriot's Point. This is the only way to get here.

The fort itself isn't physically imposing or visually impressive, but for a traveler with even a passing interest in American history, a trip to Sumter is requisite. The fort is named after Revolutionary War patriot Thomas Sumter, and its construction on an artificial island, in large part undertaken by enslaved laborers and craftspeople, began in 1829. Its 5ft-thick brick walls towered about 50ft over the water and supported several tiers of weaponry, though they were still unfinished in 1860 when Federal troops moved in.

The Fort Under Attack

On April 12, 1861, Confederate forces fired on the fort, and less than two days later the Union surrendered. The port of Charleston became a loophole in the blockade of the Atlantic coast, allowing the Confederacy to receive needed supplies and to continue exporting cotton. They held it for nearly four years, until General William T Sherman and his troops forced an evacuation in 1865. The fort was mostly unused until after WWII, when it became part of the National Monument.

Your Visit

Upon arrival, you'll disembark the ferry and gather around a national park ranger, who'll give an entertaining and efficient talk on the history of the site and its role in the Civil War. From there you'll have about an hour to wander the fort and its small museum. A map provided by the park can help you decide how to spend your time.

Fort Sumter Visitor Education Center

Getting to Fort Sumter requires hopping on a boat tour, and most of these leave from Liberty Sq, where the Fort Sumter Visitor Education Center is based. (The other jumping-off point is Patriot's Point in Mt Pleasant.) The visitor

◉ MAP P26

☎ 843-883-3123; www.nps.gov/fosu

★ Top Tips

○ If you only have time for one fortification, visit Fort Moultrie. It's cheaper, more accessible and covers more historical ground.

○ Afternoon trips to Fort Sumter tend to be less crowded.

○ Book a combo ticket online for Fort Sumter and the USS *Yorktown* at Patriot's Point ($39).

✕ Take a Break

Buy snacks on the Fort Sumter ferry boat, as there are no restaurants around. Near Fort Moultrie on Sullivan's island, Obstinate Daughter (p86) is great for seafood, and Poe's Tavern (p88) is good for hamburgers. (FYI: Edgar Allan Poe was stationed at Fort Moultrie from 1827 to 1828.)

center offers exhibits on the roots of conflict that led to the Civil War, South Carolina's secession and the war's aftermath. It's a good primer before jumping on the boat, if you've got time, and is open daily from 8:30am to 5pm.

Fort Moultrie

Although it's not as famous as Fort Sumter, **Fort Moultrie** (☎843-883-3123; www.nps.gov/fosu; 1214 Middle St, Sullivan's Island; adult/child $3/free; ⏰9am-5pm) actually offers a deeper dive into the region's coastal defense systems, as its exhibits and structures span nearly 200 years. The fort standing today is the third version of Moultrie, and a very different structure than the first, which was composed of palmetto logs that held back the British in 1776. The site of that old fort is to the west of the present-day fort.

It is at the western tip of Sullivan's Island and to get there requires wheels

Outside the Walls
Other attractions outside the walls include the site of the second Fort Moultrie, which was destroyed by a hurricane in 1801. There's also a cannon walk, which showcases

Fort Moultrie

MEUNIERD/SHUTTERSTOCK ©

artillery pieces from the Civil War, and a burial site for Seminole leader Osceola, who died at the fort in 1838. Children and dogs will love to play on the fine white sands and climb the rocks on the adjacent beach.

Inside the Fort
Inside the fort, visitors can behold a WWII harbor command post, a couple of batteries designed in the early 1900s to protect the minefield, an exhibit of the modernization of weapons in 1870, and a display of the sweeping technological changes that happened during the Civil War. There's enough here to keep you busy for several hours, particularly if you're a history buff.

Fort Moultrie Visitor Center
Across the street from the fort, the visitor center has an information desk staffed by friendly park rangers, along with a theater, a museum and a bookstore.

Definitely check out the 22-minute documentary film

An Officer & a Gentleman
Pierre Beauregard, the Confederate general who commanded the attack on Fort Sumter, had been a student of Major Robert Anderson, the Union commander defending the fort, at West Point. Communications between the two men before the siege demonstrate the utmost respect.

on Fort Moultrie and the coastal defense system. It begins every half-hour in the theater.

The museum in here can be conquered in about 30 minutes, and includes artifacts and exhibits on the American Revolution, the Civil War, WWI and WWII (the fort evolved to meet the needs of each of these conflicts).

There is also some information on the slave trade at Sullivan's Island.

Explore ✦

Beaufort & Hilton Head Island

The southern half of the South Carolina coast is a tangle of islands cut off from the mainland by inlets and tidal marshes. Here, descendants of West African slaves known as the Gullah maintain small communities in the face of resort and golf-course development. The landscape ranges from tidy stretches of shimmery, oyster-gray sand to wild, moss-shrouded maritime forests.

On Port Royal Island, darling colonial Beaufort (byoo-furt) is the second-oldest city in South Carolina, and perhaps the nation's greatest educator on the turbulent post–Civil War period. The streets are lined with gorgeous antebellum homes, restored 18th-century mansions and twisting magnolias that drip with Spanish moss. Across Port Royal Sound, upmarket Hilton Head Island is South Carolina's largest barrier island and one of America's top golf spots. It was also the first eco-planned destination in the USA.

Getting There & Around

Most people use their own wheels in the Lowcountry. Those visiting Hilton Head usually fly into Savannah/Hilton Head International Airport (p149) in Savannah, 40 miles west of the island. Beaufort is 71 miles southwest of Charleston International Airport (p149) and 46 miles northeast of Savannah/Hilton Head International Airport.

Beaufort & Hilton Head Island Map on p96

Beaufort & Hilton Head Island

Beaufort

| A | B | C | D |

BEAUFORT

Bladen St
Monson St
4
Santa Elena
History Center

Hilton Head Island
(See Main Map; 31mi)

Wilmington St
Harrington St
King St
North St
Church St
Bay St
Newcastle St
Charles St
West St
Scott St
Carteret St

8
3 Pat Conroy
Literary Center
Craven St
13
Historic
Carriage
Tours
Port Republic St
Bay St
11
Hemingway's
BUS
21
Henry C Chambers
Waterfront Park
2
14
Henry C Chambers
Waterfront Park
Woods
Memorial
Bridge

Beaufort River
Downtown
Marina

1

**SOUTH
CAROLINA**

May River

Barataria
Island

Bull
Island

Bull Creek

Calibogue
Sound
Buck
Island

Harbour Town
Lighthouse
5
Plantation
Dr

Cooper River

Pine
Island

Ramshorn Creek

Daufuskie 7
Island

New River

Greenwood Dr

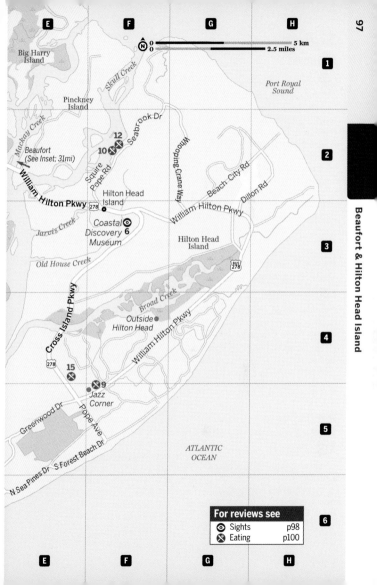

0 ____ 5 km
0 ____ 2.5 miles

Big Harry Island

Pinckney Island

Skull Creek

Port Royal Sound

Mackay Creek

Beaufort (See Inset; 31mi)

William Hilton Pkwy

12
10
Seabrook Dr

Squire Pope Rd

Hilton Head Island

278

Whooping Crane Way

Beach City Rd

Dillon Rd

William Hilton Pkwy

Jarvis Creek

Coastal Discovery Museum 6

Hilton Head Island

Old House Creek

278 BUS

Cross Island Pkwy

Broad Creek

Outside Hilton Head

William Hilton Pkwy

ATLANTIC OCEAN

278
15

9
Jazz Corner
Pope Ave

Greenwood Dr

N Sea Pines Dr   S Forest Beach Dr

For reviews see	
⊙ Sights	p98
✗ Eating	p100

Sights

Sandbar
NATURAL FEATURE

1 ⊙ MAP P96, A3

At low tide on a warm day, Beaufort's sandbar is the place to drink and be drunk. It's only about a mile south of the Henry C Chambers Waterfront Park, and people show up in all manner of watercraft, including boats, kayaks and paddle boards. They bring coolers with enough booze to last long after the tide goes out, and on some days there are even concerts performed on a floating stage. (Beaufort River)

Henry C Chambers Waterfront Park
PARK

2 ⊙ MAP P96, C2

Overlooking the bay, this iconic downtown anchor is flanked by dining options, shops and art galleries. Many of Beaufort's festivals and events are held here, and it's a really beautiful place to watch the sun dip behind the marina. (☏ 843-525-7011; Bay St)

Pat Conroy Literary Center
ARTS CENTER

3 ⊙ MAP P96, C2

Until his death in 2016, South Carolina's literary great Pat Conroy called Beaufort home. The city inspired some of his most famous works, including The Great Santini and The Prince of Tides, and this newly established literary center offers exhibits on his life and work, including his writing desk and chair, and a handwritten prologue to The Prince of Tides.

The center also hosts events including the **Pat Conroy Literary Festival** (http://patconroyliterary festival.org; 308 Charles St; day pass from $73.50; ⊙ Oct) and readings by acclaimed authors. (☏ 843-379-7025; http://patconroyliterarycenter. org; 308 Charles St; ⊙ noon-4pm Thu-Sun)

Santa Elena History Center
MUSEUM

4 ⊙ MAP P96, A1

Tucked into an old federal courthouse, this history museum tells the largely unfamiliar story of the earliest Europeans to settle in North America, and we're not talking about Jamestown.

Back in 1562 the French landed on present day Parris Island and dubbed it Charlesfort. They abandoned the site, but in 1566 the Spanish moved in and renamed it Santa Elena. This museum describes the early rivalry between these nations, and how the colonialists lived.

There's a short film to orient you before visiting the exhibits. Kids will enjoy the hands-on archaeological 'dig' for artifacts on the 1st floor. (☏ 843-379-1550; www. coastaldiscovery.org; 1501 Bay St; $10; ⊙ 10am-4pm Tue-Sat; ⏿)

Harbour Town Lighthouse

LIGHTHOUSE, MUSEUM

5 MAP P96, D5

Hilton Head's lighthouse, with the only female lighthouse keeper in North America, was built in 1970 and is prettily perched at the Harbour Town marina on the island's southern end, tucked away on Sea Pines Plantation. The 114 steps to the top are a museum, filled with Civil War artifacts, island history and regional lighthouse history, which certainly makes climbing them more interesting than otherwise. In addition to the admission, you'll pay a $6 day-pass fee for Sea Pines.

The entryway downstairs doubles as a maritime gift gallery, with nautical items and South Carolina books and memorabilia, and there's also a gift shop at the top. (www.harbourtownlighthouse. com; 149 Lighthouse Rd; adult/child $4.25/free; ⊗10am-sunset)

Coastal Discovery Museum

MUSEUM

6 ◎ MAP P96, F3

A Smithsonian Affiliate, this Hilton Head museum is well worth a trip for its exhibits highlighting the island's rich Gullah history, natural wonders and other coastal treasures. A trail system on the 62-acre property winds past ancient oak trees, lush gardens and historic buildings. The museum suggests a donation of $5. (☏843-689-6767; www.coastaldiscovery.org; 70 Honey

Henry C Chambers Waterfront Park

Horn Dr; admission free; ⏰9am-4:30pm Mon-Sat, 11am-3pm Sun)

Daufuskie Island   ISLAND

7 ◉ MAP P96, B6

For those looking for an escape just a touch less discovered than Hilton Head, this idyllic island offers a sublime day trip and a window into the Lowcountry's slower-paced past. The attractions of the island – a historical trail, a few restaurants, a couple of golf clubs, some art galleries, a winery and a rum distillery – are best visited via golf cart, the primary mode of transport on the island. Its shores are only accessible by boat.

For information about the ferry and water taxi, visit www.daufuskie islandferry.com. (www.hiltonhead island.org/daufuskie-island)

Eating

Ribaut Social Club   AMERICAN $$

8 🍴 MAP P96, C2

A refined yet homey Lowcountry restaurant, set in the refurbished mansion **Anchorage 1770** (📞877-951-1770; https://anchorage1770. com; 1103 Bay St; r $235-375; ❄️🛜) that once belonged to Admiral Beardslee (and named after his boisterous gentlemen's club).

The executive chef brings a personal touch to regional, seasonal dishes, and excels with seared sea scallops with Carolina gold rice and a tender duck breast in a pomegranate bourbon glaze.

Grab a pre-dinner drink in the parlor or on the 4th-floor terrace overlooking the Port Royal Sound, and don't miss the fabulous Sunday brunch.

Reservations are a great idea. (📞877-951-1770; https://anchorage 1770.com/dining.aspx; 1103 Bay St; mains $20-32; ⏰5-7:30pm Wed-Sat, 11am-2pm Sun)

Java Burrito   MEXICAN $

9 🍴 MAP P96, F5

Like a sustainably tricked-out Chipotle, this family-owned, farm-to-table burrito Eden is impossible not to love, which is why in-the-know Hilton Head islanders are addicted to it. Choose your method (burrito, bowl, taco etc), choose your protein (chicken, steak, veggies, eggs,

Food Scene

Beaufort has a smaller culinary scene than Charleston, but it isn't short on Lowcountry scrumptiousness or fresh seafood. A handful of good restaurants offer outdoor dining with views of the river, and the elegant Ribaut Social Club leads the pack.

Meanwhile, Hilton Head is known for its fresh Lowcountry seafood and an overall resistance to chain restaurants. The island thrives on locally owned, independently operated restaurants specializing in fresh-off-the-boat fish, shrimp, oysters and crab.

Worth a Trip: St Helena, Parris and Hunting Islands

Within day-tripping distance from Beaufort, a cluster of marshy, rural islands offers an enticing amalgam of history, culture and nature, with a splash of Marine Corps action and some super-tasty shrimp burgers to boot.

Across the bridge to the east, **St Helena Island** is the heart of Gullah country, where the descendants of slaves have meticulously preserved their language and culture, and where two Reconstruction Era National Monuments were established by President Obama in 2017. For a deeper appreciation of all things Gullah, there's the longstanding **Gullah-N-Geechie Mahn Tours** (☏843-838-7516; www.gullahngeechietours.net; 16 Penn Center Circle W; per person from $32, minimum 2 people; ⊙tours 9am, 11:30am, 1:45pm Mon-Sat).

Farther east, on **Hunting Island**, you'll find **Hunting Island State Park** (☏843-838-2011; www.southcarolinaparks.com/huntingisland; 2555 Sea Island Pkwy; adult/child 6-15yr $5/3; ⊙park 6am-6pm, to 9pm Mar-Sep, visitor center 9am-5pm Mon-Fri, 11am-5pm Sat & Sun, nature center 9am-5pm Tue-Sat, daily Jun-Aug) – one of the state's most breathtaking coastal parks – and perhaps a shark tooth.

To the south, **Parris Island** features a Marine Corps training ground and **museum** (☏843-228-2951; www.parrisislandmuseum.com; 111 Panama St; admission free; ⊙10am-4:30pm), and an archaeological site where the country's first European settlers landed.

And for kayak and stand up paddling (SUP) enthusiasts, tour company **Higher Ground** (☏843-379-4327; https://highergroundoutfitters.com; 95 Factory Creek Ct, Lady's Island; tours per person from $50, rental kayak or SUP half/full day $40/60; ⊙10am-6pm Mon-Sat, 1-4pm Sun) has rental gear and trips out of Sea Island. As if all that isn't enough, the sweeping views from the bridges connecting these lowland isles are beyond postcard-pretty.

Should you get hungry, head for one of the roadside seafood places or Gullah restaurants (both are easy to come by on St Helena and Lady's Islands).

If you're headed to Hunting Island State Park, grab snacks and coffee at **Carolina Cider Company & Superior Coffee** (www.carolinaciderco.com; 507 Sea Island Pkwy, St Helena Island; ⊙8am-6pm Mon-Sat, from 8:30am Sun, open longer hours in summer) or a famous shrimp burger at **Shrimp Shack** (☏843-838-2962; 1929 Sea Island Pkwy; mains from $3, shrimp burgers $8; ⊙11am-2pm Mon-Sat).

Activities & Tours

Golf, bicycling and dolphin-watching are the prime activities on Hilton Head, and **Outside Hilton Head** (Map p96, F4; ☏800-686-6996; www.outsidehiltonhead.com; 1 Shelter Cove Lane; ⏱8am-6pm summer, shorter hours rest of year) is the big water sports outfitter. Beaufort's got plenty of water sports, too, along with a plethora of tours.

Historic carriage tours (☏843-524-2900, 843-476-7789; 1002 Bay St; tour $23; ⏱hours vary) are a great way to get acquainted with Beaufort's history. **Pat Conroy's Beaufort Tour** (☏843-838-2746; www.beauforttoursllc.com; adult/child 4-12yr $30/15; ⏱2pm Thu-Sun) is highly recommended for fans of the author. Daredevils will enjoy **Vintage Biplane Tours** (☏904-910-6369; www.beaufortbiplanetours. com; 30-min flight $200; ⏱11am-6pm).

local fish etc), choose your fixings (rice, beans, queso etc), then die happy.

From the Mexican dishes to the breakfast sandwiches to the parfait, everything is antibiotic- and hormone-free, locally and sustainably sourced, and tasty as hell. But that's not all! It doubles as an excellent coffee bar and has beer, wine, great peach margaritas and even champagne! (☏843-842-5282; www.javaburritoco.com; 1000 William Hilton Pkwy; mains $7-14; ⏱7:30am-9pm Mon-Sat; 🛜)

Hudson's   SEAFOOD $$

10 ✖ MAP P96, F2

Hilton Head's go-to seafood shack is a doozy, with a wonderful dock-side deck on the water that brims with revelry (old-time islanders stick to the cozy indoor bar), all of which is centered on the bounties of the sea. Anything with shrimp,

(seasonal) soft-shell crab or fresh oysters (they cultivate and harvest their own seasonally) will woo you.

If it's not from these waters, it's not plated. And, incidentally, they might have the South's best hush puppies. (☏843-681-2772; www. hudsonsonthedocks.com; 1 Hudson Rd; lunch $9-24, dinner $14-34; ⏱11am-3pm & 5-9pm; 🛜)

Old Bull Tavern   GASTROPUB $$

11 ✖ MAP P96, D2

The Old Bull Tavern offers some of the tastiest food and cocktails in Beaufort, with a wood-fired pizza oven and low-lit, worldly aesthetic to boot. The menu changes daily but always features playful American and European comfort dishes, prepared with fresh seasonal ingredients, often with a clever twist. Start with the wasabi deviled eggs and prosciutto, and continue with the braised lamb shank.

Wash it all down with a bourbon flight or a Yemassee cooler (rum, Aperol, lemon juice, blackberry shrub, orange bitters and soda). (☎843-379-2855; http://oldbulltavern.com; 205 West St; mains $13-18; ⏲5-9:30pm Tue-Thu, to 10pm Fri & Sat)

Skull Creek Dockside Restaurant
SEAFOOD $$

12 ✖ MAP P96, F2

Set in a renovated old river house, the latest addition to Hilton Head's dining scene raises the (already high) bar for seafood with its mouthwatering amalgam of American, Italian and Southern dishes. Think heaping plates of meat-heavy crab cakes, scallops seared in citrus butter and colossal stuffed shrimp, paired with

sides like pimento-cheese grits and creamy collard greens.

The dining room is elegantly adorned in reclaimed wood with natural accents, and offers giant windows overlooking a newly refurbished dock. But dramatic warm-weather sunsets simply must be enjoyed from the covered patio or the outdoor bar. The wine list is excellent. (☎843-785-3625; www.docksidehhi.com; 2 Hudson Rd; mains $15-29; ⏲11am-10pm Mon-Thu, to 11pm Fri & Sat, 10am-10pm Sun)

Lowcountry Produce
SOUTHERN US $

13 ✖ MAP P96, D2

A fantastic Beaufort cafe and market for picnic rations such as pies, housemade relishes, local cheeses

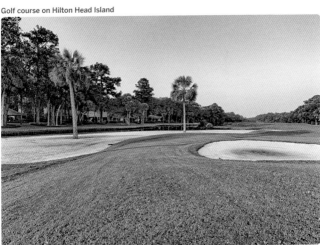
Golf course on Hilton Head Island

and all kinds of Lowcountry-spun awesomeness (including a bizarre but wildly popular cream-cheese lasagna). Or eat in and indulge in an Oooey Gooey, a grilled pimento-cheese sandwich with bacon and garlic-pepper jelly (one hot mess!), or a tasty crab-cake sandwich with brussels-sprouts slaw.

It's a madhouse here on weekends, for good reason. And the Bloody Marys are fabulous. (📞843-322-1900; www.lowcountry produce.com; 302 Carteret St;

Why Is Beaufort So Well Preserved?

In November 1861, Union forces prevailed in the Battle of Port Royal, laying siege to Confederate forts on Hilton Head Island and St Helena Island. When slave owners in Beaufort caught wind of this, they all skipped town in what a newspaper columnist famously dubbed Beaufort's 'Great Skedaddle.'

As tour guides tell it, white people left so fast that Union soldiers found half-eaten suppers on the tables. There was fear of a revolt, because back then Beaufort's population was 85% enslaved people. These newly freed African Americans were left behind to tend to the homes, all of which remain standing today. For this reason, Beaufort is an exceptional place to visit not only to view magnificent antebellum homes, but also to learn about the Reconstruction Era and the culture of the Gullah people, who are descendants of the ex-slaves.

After the war, Beaufort's infrastructure was largely converted into hospitals where soldiers and former slaves got medical care. Over on St Helena Island, Penn School was established to educate ex-slaves and provide social services and employment assistance. Dar-rah Hall, the oldest standing structure on the school grounds, is one of four sites that in 2017 was named a Reconstruction Era National Monument by President Obama. Others include the Brick Church, where classes were held, the Old Beaufort Fire House, a social and economic hub of the time, and Camp Saxton in Port Royal, where 5000 African Americans (many of whom were ex-slaves) were recruited to join the Union army.

Notable figures with connections to Beaufort include Harriet Tubman, conductor of the Underground Railroad, who worked here to liberate slaves and recruit them into the army. On carriage tours, visitors also pass the former home of Robert Smalls, an ex-slave who commandeered a Confederate ship, turned it over to the Union and became the period's most inspiring African American politician.

breakfast $9-15, sandwiches $10-18; ⏰8am-3pm; 📶)

Plums
SOUTHERN US $

14 🍴 MAP P96, C2

A solid waterfront bistro in Beaufort serving creative Lowcountry cuisine whipped up with local, seasonal ingredients. Great sandwiches, salads and seafood, and the shrimp-and-crab dip served with warm pretzel-y bread is a mouth's dream. (📞843-525-1946; http://plumsrestaurant.com; 904 Bay St; mains $10-15; ⏰11am-9pm)

Red Fish
SEAFOOD $$$

15 🍴 MAP P96, E4

Equal parts bottle shop, art gallery and intimate seafooder, Red Fish hosts power-lunch cronies by day and Hilton Head islander foodies by night, both of whom come for hook-to-table seafood (a co-owner's husband does the fishing himself), paired with excellent Californian and Oregonian wines. Start with the baked pimento-cheese appetizer, then go for whatever's freshest, which

Drinking & Nightlife

Beaufort is called a 'two-liver town,' meaning you'll need two livers to do this place right.

The **Sandbar** (p98) is the drinking spot of choice on warm days, and **Hemingway's** (📞843-521-4480; www.hemingways.org; 920 Bay St; ⏰10am-2am; 📶) is a hub regardless of the weather. Locals you have just met may invite you along: just go.

On Hilton Head Island, most of the independent nightlife is concentrated on the south end in an area known as the 'Bermuda Triangle.' **Jazz Corner** (Map p96, F5; 📞843-842-8620; www.thejazzcorner.com; 1000 William Hilton Pkwy; ⏰6-11pm) is also a great spot for live music and a martini.

is often prepped with Asian and Latin touches. (📞843-686-3388; www.redfishofhiltonhead.com; 8 Archer Rd; mains $24-39; ⏰11:30am-2pm & 5-9pm Mon-Sat; 📶)

Explore ⊛

Historic District & Forsyth Park

Fringed by Forsyth Park to its south, Savannah's Historic District – the largest National Historic Landmark District in the country – is home to 22 gorgeous squares that serve as a backdrop for exquisite 18th- and 19th-century homes, fascinating museums and monuments, and world-class restaurants, all enveloped by a dazzling canopy of Spanish-moss-laden live oak trees.

The sights of Savannah's Historic District are among the best in the country. Monuments, museums and grand homes will keep you wandering in wonder. The district is arranged in a grid, making it easy to walk from one end to the other, with Forsyth Park at the southern edge near the Victorian District, and River St to the far north. President St is the eastern boundary and Martin Luther King Jr Blvd is the western, where you'll find the visitor center.

Getting There & Around

The **JMR Transit Center** (610 W Oglethorpe Ave) just west of the Historic District is the city's local transport hub. You can catch the free 'dot' line for rides all around the area and to Forsyth Park. Taxis, pedicabs and bikes are also great ways to get around if you're staying close by.

Historic District & Forsyth Park Map on p112

Cathedral of St John the Baptist (p115) F11PHOTO/SHUTTERSTOCK ©

Top Experience 📷
Get Outdoors at Forsyth Park

Beloved of locals and visitors alike, Forsyth Park is abuzz with events and activities year-round. The sprawling green lawns, historic monuments and majestic fountain form the heart and soul of downtown Savannah's outdoor life – it's the place to come to be active, lay in the sun and have a picnic, or simply stroll around the paths and take in all its splendor.

◎ MAP P112, C8

admission free

Inspired Design

Developed in the 1840s on 10 acres of land donated to the city by Savannah scholar-diplomat William Hodgson, Forsyth Park was part of Oglethorpe's original vision for the city and was expanded after Georgia governor John Forsyth donated an additional 20 acres that tripled the size of the park. In conceiving Forsyth's layout, Bavarian landscape designer William Bischoff took cues from the French. He was inspired by urban-renewal efforts taking place in Paris that featured neighborhoods radiating out from a central green space. In 1858 a fountain was installed and over the years, monuments to commemorate historic events in Savannah have been added, as well as a Garden of Fragrance for the blind, an outdoor amphitheater, a playground and tennis courts.

The Famous Founders

Forsyth's central fountain is the park's crown jewel and has become a distinctive icon of Savannah – but it's not quite as unique as people think.

When the fountain was decided upon in 1858, city council appointed a committee to choose a design...from a catalog. The design, simply known as 'No 5,' was one of a few elaborate options featured in a catalog of ornamental ironwork by Janes, Beebe & Company of New York. Modeled after a fountain designed by Michel Joseph Napoleon Lienard and cast by the JPV Andre Iron Foundry in Paris, its inspiration was sourced during the Great Exhibition of 1851 at the Crystal Palace in London's Hyde Park after a Janes, Beebe & Company representative was sent to research the manufacturing of garden ornaments.

One thing sets Forsyth's fountain apart, though: every St Patrick's Day, its waters are ceremoniously dyed green.

★ **Top Tips**

○ On Saturdays, check out the farmers market on the south end of the park.

○ Pick a patch of grass on the north side of the park near the fountain for more shade and a bit of an intimate feel.

○ Enjoy the park by day or night; just don't linger past midnight.

✕ **Take a Break**

The Sentient Bean (p130) is across the street from the park's south entrance on Park Ave – it has great coffee and tasty, healthy food.

Walking Tour 🥾

Savannah's Squares

One of the great joys of visiting Savannah is simply walking around the historic district amid some of the most beautiful residential architecture in the country. The city's original layout is an inspiring bit of urban planning: four open squares, each one ensconced within four residential and four civic blocks, a pattern that has repeated itself as Savannah has grown.

Walk Facts

Start: Forsyth Park

End: Johnson Sq

Length: 1¾ miles, two hours

❶ Forsyth Park

Begin this leisurely stroll at the south entrance of **Forsyth Park** (p108) at Bull St and Park Ave. Head north along the main thoroughfare and arrive at the iconic fountain for an obligatory photo op.

❷ Monterey Square

Stay north on Bull St toward the intersection of Wayne St, where a tall monument topped with a statue of General Casimir Pulaski greets you in **Monterey Sq**, one of Savannah's most picturesque.

❸ Mercer-Williams House

The **Mercer-Williams House** (p114), setting of the novel and film *Midnight in the Garden of Good and Evil*, faces its west side – pop in to hear the harrowing history of what went down inside Savannah's most famous haunted house.

❹ Chippewa Square

Chippewa Sq sits smack in the middle of the Historic District, with a bronze statue of Savannah founder James Oglethorpe overseeing all the action from the center.

❺ Wright Square

Keep truckin' north on Bull St, past Oglethorpe Ave, to York St and arrive at **Wright Sq**. This was the second square constructed in Savannah and is the burial site of Tomochichi, the Yamacraw tribe leader who befriended Oglethorpe and helped him establish the colony.

❻ Telfair Square

Head west on York St for two blocks to **Telfair Sq**. You won't find any monuments with a contentious backstory in this square, but you will find creative inspiration all around it – both the **Telfair Academy** (p114) and the **Jepson Center for the Arts** (p114) sit on Barnard St.

❼ Ellis Square

Continue north on Barnard St and cross over Broughton St, downtown's main commercial drag, toward Congress St to arrive at **Ellis Sq**. It was a center for commerce from the 1730s through the 1950s, and in the 1850s it housed a slave market.

❽ Johnson Sq

Head back east down St Julian St toward Bull St and end the journey at **Johnson Sq**, Savannah's first and largest square.

✕ Take a Break

Cool off at **Leopold's Ice Cream** (p118), the classic American dessert parlor where tutti-frutti was invented.

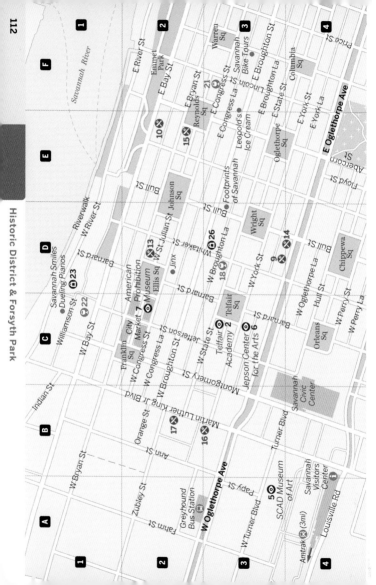

Historic District & Forsyth Park

Savannah River

Riverwalk

Savannah Smiles
Dueling Pianos

American
Prohibition
Museum

City
Market 7

Ellis Sq

Jinx

Johnson
Sq

Footprints
of Savannah

Warren
Sq

Savannah
Bike Tours

Leopold's
Ice Cream

Reynolds
Sq

Columbia
Sq

Oglethorpe
Sq

Wright
Sq

Telfair
Sq

Telfair
Academy 2

Jepson Center
for the Arts 6

Franklin
Sq

Wright
Sq

Chippewa
Sq

Orleans
Sq

Savannah
Civic Center

Greyhound
Bus Station

SCAD Museum
of Art 5

Savannah
Visitors
Center

Antrak (3mi)

Historic District & Forsyth Park

For reviews see

◆	Top Experiences	p108
◉	Sights	p114
✖	Eating	p116
⬤	Drinking	p118
⬤	Shopping	p119

200 m
0.1 miles

HISTORIC DISTRICT

Colonial Park Cemetery

Cathedral of St John the Baptist ◉ 8

✖ 11

Lafayette Sq

Flannery O'Connor Childhood Home ◉ 4

Sorrel Weed House 3 ◉

◉ 20

📍 24

◉ 25

19 ⬤

Madison Sq

Pulaski Sq

Chatham Sq

Mercer-Williams House ◉ 1

✖ 12

Monterey Sq

Calhoun Sq

Whitefield Sq

Troup Sq

Forsyth Park ◆

Sights

Mercer-Williams House
HISTORIC BUILDING

1 ◉ MAP P112, C6

Although Jim Williams, the Savannah art dealer portrayed by Kevin Spacey in the film version of *Midnight in the Garden of Good and Evil,* died back in 1990, his infamous mansion didn't become a museum until 2004. You're not allowed to visit the upstairs, where Williams' family still lives, but the downstairs is an interior decorator's fantasy. (☎912-236-6352; www.mercerhouse.com; 429 Bull St; adult/student $12.50/8; ⏱10:30am-4:10pm Mon-Sat, noon-4pm Sun)

Telfair Academy
MUSEUM

2 ◉ MAP P112, C3

Considered Savannah's top art museum, the historic Telfair family mansion is filled with 19th-century American art and silver and a smattering of European pieces. The home itself is gorgeous and sunrise-hued – an artifact in its own right that wows visitors. (☎912-790-8800; www.telfair.org/visit/telfair; 121 Barnard St; adult/child $20/15; ⏱noon-5pm Sun & Mon, 10am-5pm Tue-Sat)

Sorrel Weed House
HOUSE

3 ◉ MAP P112, D5

Fans of the paranormal can get their thrills at one of Savannah's spookiest mansions – the ghost tours are genuinely creepy and the grounds hauntingly beautiful.

(☎912-257-2223; www.sorrelweed house.com; 6 W Harris St; ⏱10am-11:30pm)

Flannery O'Connor Childhood Home
MUSEUM

4 ◉ MAP P112, E6

This stone row house on Lafayette Sq is where the literary great was born in 1925 and lived until she was 13. Her second short-story collection won the National Book Award in 1972 – eight years after she died. (☎912-233-6014; www.flanneryoconnorhome.org; 207 E Charlton St; adult/student $6/5; ⏱1-4pm Fri-Wed, closed Thu)

SCAD Museum of Art
MUSEUM

5 ◉ MAP P112, A3

Architecturally striking, this brick, steel, concrete and glass longhouse delivers your contemporary-art fix. There are groovy, creative sitting areas inside and out, and a number of rotating and visiting exhibitions that showcase some of the most impressive talents within the contemporary-art world. (www.scadmoa.org; 601 Turner Blvd; adult/child under 14yr $10/free; ⏱10am-5pm Tue, Wed, Fri & Sat, to 8pm Thu, noon-5pm Sun)

Jepson Center for the Arts
GALLERY

6 ◉ MAP P112, C3

Designed by the great Moshe Safdie, and looking pretty darn space-age by Savannah's standards, the JCA focuses on 20th- and

21st-century art. Be on the lookout for wandering scads of SCAD students (ha!) and temporary exhibitions covering topics from race to art in virtual-reality video games. (JCA; ☎912-790-8800; www.telfair.org/visit/jepson; 207 W York St; adult/child $20/15; ⏰noon-5pm Sun & Mon, 10am-5pm Tue-Sat; ♿)

American Prohibition Museum MUSEUM

7 ◉ MAP P112, C2

Learn about the history of prohibition in the US in this spirited museum, the only one of its kind in the country. Exhibits feature live actors, films, animated portraits and detailed wax figures, and you can round out your visit with a tipple on the top floor at Up, the museum's speakeasy. (☎912-220-1249; www.americanprohibition museum.com; 209 W St Julian St; adult/child $13/10; ⏰10am-5pm)

Cathedral of St John the Baptist CHURCH

8 ◉ MAP P112, E5

Completed in 1896 but destroyed by fire two years later, this impressive cathedral, reopened in 1912, features stunning stained-glass transept windows from Austria depicting Christ's ascension into heaven, as well as ornate Station of the Cross woodcarvings from Bavaria. (☎912-233-4709; www.savannahcathedral.org; 222 E Harris St; ⏰Mass 7:30am & noon Mon-Fri, noon & 5:30pm Sat, 8am, 10am & 11:30am Sun, in Latin 1pm Sun)

Sorrel Weed House

NATALIA BRATSLAVSKY/SHUTTERSTOCK ©

Historic District Tours

Learn about the side of Savannah that didn't make it into the history books with Vaughnette Goode-Walker's **Footprints of Savannah** (Map p112, D3; 912-695-3872; www.footprintsof savannah.com; tours begin in Wright Sq; adult/child $20/7; daily tours 10am), a 1½-hour walking tour that highlights the city's rich and complex African American history. Or if you prefer to learn on wheels, **Savannah Bike Tours** (Map p112, F3; 912-704-4043; www. savannahbiketours.com; 41 Habersham St; tours $25; varies by season) offers two-hour cycling excursions over easy flat terrain on its fleet of cruisers.

Eating

Husk Savannah   SOUTHERN US $$$

9 MAP P112, D3

After acclaimed success with Charleston, Nashville and Greenville locations, celebrity-chef Sean Brock brings Husk's hyper-local, agriculturally driven Southern food sorcery to Savannah. This outpost is the only one boasting a raw seafood bar and is the biggest of all, set in a historic, three-story space that hosts 200 people. Like all locations, the daily menu depends on what's locally available. (912-349-2600; www.husksavannah.com;

12 W Oglethorpe Ave; mains $25-36; 5-10pm Sun-Thu, to 11pm Fri & Sat)

Treylor Park   SOUTHERN US $

10 MAP P112, E2

All the hip young things pack into this 'Treylor Park,' which revels in a retro-chic, Airstream aesthetic. The food? Southern classics simply done well: fried chicken on a biscuit with sausage gravy and spicy collard greens, or a grilled apple-pie sandwich. Take your pick and wash it down with an excellent cocktail in the warmly lit courtyard. (888-873-9567, 912-495-5557; www. treylorparksavannah.com; 115 E Bay St; mains $6-14; noon-midnight Mon-Wed, from 10am Sat & Sun)

Fox & Fig   VEGAN $

11 MAP P112, E6

A range of internationally inspired dishes get plant-based treatments at this charming cafe. Try the seared Southern seitan (wheat gluten) with French toast if you want a fix of something more indulgent but could do without the chicken-fried guilt. (912-297-6759; www.foxandfigcafe.com; 321 Habersham St; mains $7-16; 8am-9pm Tue-Sun, to 3pm Mon)

Mrs Wilkes Dining Room   SOUTHERN US $$

12 MAP P112, C6

The line outside can begin as early as 8am at this first-come, first-served Southern comfort-food institution. Once the lunch bell rings and you are seated family-style, the kitchen unloads on you: fried chicken, beef stew, meatloaf, cheese potatoes, collard greens, black-eyed peas, mac 'n' cheese, rutabaga, candied yams, squash casserole, creamed corn *and* biscuits. It's like Thanksgiving and the Last Supper rolled into one massive feast, chased with sweet tea. (www.mrswilkes.com; 107 W Jones St; lunch adult/child $22/11; ⏰11am-2pm Mon-Fri Feb-Dec; 👶)

Little Duck   DINER $

13 🗺 MAP P112, D2

Classic diner fare gets reimagined in this bright, airy, art-deco-inspired space. We love its dedicated grilled-cheese menu, where you can scale up the traditional variety with Gruyère and Havarti, or go all out with indulgent ingredients such as duck or smoked salmon – plus a bowl of tomato soup, as you do. Tacos, bowls and breakfast are all top notch. (📞912-235-6773; www.littleduckdiner.com; 150 W Saint Julian St; mains $8-15; ⏰10am-3pm & 5-10pm Mon-Fri, 9am-10pm Sat & Sun)

Collins Quarter   CAFE $$

14 🗺 MAP P112, D4

This wildly popular newcomer is Australian-owned and turns Aussie-roasted Brooklyn coffee into beloved flat whites and long blacks. Beyond Savannah's best coffee, it serves excellent fusion fare, including a drool-inducing brisket burger. There's booze too! (📞912-777-4147; www.thecollinsquarter.com; 151 Bull St;

dinner mains $17-32; ⏰6:30am-5pm Mon, to noon Tue, to 10pm Wed-Sun; 📶)

Olde Pink House   SOUTHERN US $$$

15 🗺 MAP P112, E2

Classic Southern food done upscale in one of Savannah's most consistently great restaurants. Our favorite appetizer is the Southern sushi – shrimp and grits rolled in a coconut-crusted nori roll. Dine in the slender digs upstairs, or go underground to the fabulous tavern where the piano player rumbles and the room is cozy, funky and perfect. The building is a 1771 landmark. (📞912-232-4286; 23 Abercorn St; mains $15-43; ⏰11am-2:30pm, 5-10:30pm, closed lunch Sun & Mon)

Prohibition   AMERICAN $$$

16 🗺 MAP P112, B3

This sleek, dimly lit throwback restaurant and bar in a speakeasy style serves upmarket small plates, hearty entrées and bespoke cocktails for lunch, brunch and dinner. There's a stage for live bands, and a Sunday supper club is in the works. (📞912-200-9255; www.prohibitionsavannah.com; 125 Martin Luther King Jr Blvd; dinner mains $15-36; ⏰11am-2:30pm, 5pm-1am)

The Grey   MODERN AMERICAN $$$

17 🗺 MAP P112, B2

A wonderfully retro makeover of the 1960s Greyhound Bus Terminal gives us one of Savannah's culinary darlings, where

Famous Ice Cream 🍽️

The classically American **Leopold's Ice Cream** (Map p112, F3; ☎912-234-4442; www.leopolds icecream.com; 212 E Broughton St; scoops $4-5.50; ⏱11am-10pm Sun-Thu, to 11pm Fri & Sat; 🛜) has been scooping up its creamy Greek recipes since 1919. Tuttifrutti was invented here, but we dig the coconut, ginger, and honey and almond cream.

chef Mashama Bailey's 'Port City Southern' cuisine is a delightful, immigrant-infused take on local grub. Bearded hipsters work the best seats in the house, around the U-shaped centerpiece bar, where scrumptious lamb shoulder and a gargantuan pork shank are standouts. Reservations essential. (☎912-662-5999; www. thegreyrestaurant.com; 109 Martin Luther King Jr Blvd; mains $14-38; ⏱5:30-10pm Sun & Tue-Thu, to 11pm Fri & Sat; 🛜)

Drinking

El-Rocko Lounge   COCKTAIL BAR

18 🚇 MAP P112, D3

One step in the door and you feel the '70s-inspired swank, but then realize the vibe – in true Savannah fashion – is absolutely chill. Friendly barkeeps mix fancy cocktails while DJs keep the energy high and dance moves steady with diverse jams on vinyl. The crowd is superhip but delightfully unpretentious, and the owner is as rad as they come. (☎912-495-5808; www.elrockolounge.com; 117 Whitaker St; ⏱5pm-3am Mon-Sat)

Artillery   COCKTAIL BAR

19 🚇 MAP P112, D5

Talented mixologists craft novel, quality cocktails in this opulent space where elements of 19th-century eclecticism and romanticism meld with modern design touches. To drink here, abide by the house rules: no hats, sandals, tank tops, noisy phones, or shots. The signature Artillery Punch – a concoction of rye whiskey, gin, brandy and rum – packs a powerful punch. Sip slowly. (www. artillerybar.com; 307 Bull St; ⏱4pm-midnight Mon-Sat)

Original Pinkie Masters   BAR

20 🚇 MAP P112, D5

Cheap, cash-only drinks and great people-watching make this hometown dive the best in town. It's far away enough from the River St ruckus, but easy enough to walk (err, stumble) to when you're ready to close out the night with the locals. (☎912-999-7106; www. theoriginalsavannah.com; 318 Drayton St; ⏱3pm-3am Mon-Thu, noon-3am Fri & Sat)

Abe's on Lincoln   BAR

21 🚇 MAP P112, F3

Pop back a beer or 10 with SCAD students and locals at this dark, dank, all-wood bar. Abe's on Lincoln attracts an eclectic crowd that stares through boozy goggles at whatever weird behavior the bartenders are inevitably tolerating that night. Good times. (☏912-349-0525; www.abesonlincoln.com; 17 Lincoln St; ⏱4pm-3am Mon-Sat)

Rocks on the Roof BAR

22 📍 MAP P112, C1

The expansive rooftop bar at the Bohemian Hotel is breezy and fun. It's at its best when the weather is fine and the fire pit is glowing. (☏912-721-3821; www.bohemianhotelsavannah.com/dining/lounge; 102 W Bay St, Bohemian Hotel; ⏱11am-midnight Sun-Thu, to 1am Fri & Sat; 🛜)

Shopping

Books on Bay BOOKS

23 🔒 MAP P112, D1

Junkies of that old-book smell will get a great fix at this quaint shop specializing in titles that date from the 17th century through the 1920s. Find 1st-edition runs of classics and works from literary greats, plus poetry collections, foreign manuscripts, religious and political texts and more. (☏912-236-7115; www.booksonbay.com; 224 W Bay St; ⏱10am-6pm)

ShopSCAD ARTS & CRAFTS

24 🔒 MAP P112, D6

All the wares at this funky, kitschy boutique are designed by students, faculty and alumni of

Olde Pink House (p117)

Understanding the Early History of Savannah

Georgia's history as one of the original 13 colonies began when James Oglethorpe and a group of inmate settlers sailed from England to Yamacraw Bluff on the banks of the Savannah River.

Early Land Disputes

In 1700 Spain, England and France all laid claim to the land that is now Georgia, deeming it 'the debatable land.' But it was the English who established the colony of Carolina in 1663 and began trading with tribes along the Savannah River. In 1712 the colony of Carolina was divided in two, North and South, and three years later the Yamassee tribe revolted against the English, resulting in the deaths of a large number of settlers. Though the revolt was abandoned and the Yamassee fled to Florida, it became apparent that some kind of 'buffer zone' between South Carolina and Florida was necessary.

There were several plans put forth, but all failed until James Oglethorpe came along. He was a young, visionary member of English Parliament who became concerned with the subhuman conditions of England's debtors' prisons after a friend of his died in one. To address the issue, he developed an idealistic plan: take the pressure off overcrowded debtors' prisons by bringing inmates to the New World to establish the buffer colony south of South Carolina. By 1732 Oglethorpe and a group of supporters convinced King George to approve the plan for the colony of Georgia to be settled on the banks south of the Savannah River.

The Establishment of Savannah

With an official charter issued, Oglethorpe and 114 colonists departed England aboard the *Anne* on November 16, 1732. After a three-month voyage, they arrived first in South Carolina where they negotiated permission to settle from Yamacraw tribe chief Tomochichi. The settlers then sailed through the mouth of the Savannah River and disembarked at Yamacraw Bluff on February 12, 1733. The city was founded on that date, and named Savannah.

Oglethorpe soon began work on plans for the city, along with co-planner William Bull. Loosely based on London as a model, it featured wards built around central squares in a grid. Trust lots for public buildings and churches were added on the east and west sides of the squares, and tithing lots for settlers' homes were laid out on the north and south sides; 22 of the original 24 squares still exist today.

Savannah's prestigious college of art and design. There are a lot of awesome finds to be uncovered. (📞912-525-5180; www.shopscad.com; 340 Bull St; 🕐9am-5:30pm Mon-Fri, 10am-6pm Sat, noon-5pm Sun)

Satchel
FASHION & ACCESSORIES

25 🔒 MAP P112, D5

Handbag obsessives should definitely duck into Satchel, owned and operated by the designer herself. She also manufactures her own goods and is a patron of all things design in Savannah. (📞912-233-1008; www.shopsatchel. com; 4 E Liberty St; 🕐10am-6pm Mon-Sat, 11am-3pm Sun)

Savannah Bee Company
FOOD

26 🔒 MAP P112, D3

This internationally renowned honey dreamland is one of Savannah's must-stops. Expect artisanal honey of infinite variety, and

Where to Hear Music

At **Savannah Smiles Dueling Pianos** (Map p112, C1; 📞912-527-6453; www.savannahsmiles duelingpianos.com; 314 Williamson St; 🕐7pm-3am Wed-Sat), patrons decide what's played on the stage, and the party crowd comes from far and wide. **Jinx** (Map p112, D2; 📞912-236-2281; www. facebook.com/thejinx912; 127 W Congress St; 🕐4pm-3am) is another good slice of odd-duck Savannah nightlife, and is popular with students, townies, musicians and anyone else who has a thing for dive-y watering holes with live music.

limitless free tastings. (📞912-233-7873; www.savannahbee.com; 104 W Broughton St; 🕐10am-7pm Mon-Sat, 11am-6pm Sun)

Explore ⊛

Midtown & the Victorian District

The residential architecture is astounding in this area, which was Savannah's first suburb and today is abuzz with a vibrant arts community and up-and-coming businesses. Admire the majestic homes from Forsyth Park to Victory Dr, the area's grand, palm-tree-lined avenue, and explore the galleries, museums, shops and restaurants that are shaping Savannah's local creative economy.

Bull St is the main artery running through this area, with Laurel Grove Cemetery being the sight furthest west, just on the edge of the Victorian District. Daffin Park is all the way east down Victory Dr, just before you approach East Savannah. Most sights, such as Starland, right in the center, are easy to navigate by foot; beyond that, a car or bike is the way to roll.

Getting There & Around

The Victorian District is easily walkable, but if venturing to Midtown, bike, car or bus may be best. Bus lines 4, 11, 14, 27 and 28 all run from the **JMR Transit Center** (610 W Oglethorpe Ave) downtown to points further south, passing right through this area.

Midtown & the Victorian District Map on p126

Victorian District NORTHFORKLIGHT/GETTY IMAGES ©

Top Experience 📸

Investigate Times Past at the Laurel Grove Cemetery

◉ MAP P126, A4

2101 Kollock St

🕗 8am-5pm

While it may not have as much pop-culture hype and natural beauty surrounding it as Bonaventure does, Laurel Grove Cemetery is worth a visit for its spectacular monuments and rich history. Developed in 1850 as area cemeteries reached capacity, it served as the city's primary burial ground; the graves of many significant people throughout Savannah's history can be seen here.

A Necropolis Divided

With two separate entrances, Laurel Grove is divided into two sections, north and south, by a highway. But more than a road divides them – Laurel Grove North was exclusively for white people, and Laurel Grove South for Black people.

The land that forms Laurel Grove today was once the Springfield Plantation, owned by one of Savannah's early colonists. Four acres of the original cemetery (the lowest, ill-drained point in a natural gorge, furthest from the city) was designated for the city's African American population, both free and enslaved. This was to replace the original graveyard in present-day Whitefield and Calhoun Sqs, which prevented southward expansion of the city. The acreage was then increased to 15, and doubled a few years later; the present allotment of 90 acres is roughly the same as Laurel Grove North.

Here Rests Savannah Society

Many notable Savannahians have been interred in both sections of Laurel Grove. On the north side, the most famed is Juliette Gordon Low, founder of the Girl Scouts of the USA, and more than 1500 Confederate soldiers are buried in a section devoted entirely to Civil War servicemen. In the south cemetery are graves of slaves and other African Americans who played an important role in the community's history, including Andrew Bryan, founder of the First African Baptist Church, and WW Law, a prominent leader in Savannah's Civil Rights movement.

All the plots in Laurel Grove North were sold off during the 1860s, but deceased Savannah residents continue to be buried in Laurel Grove South today.

★ **Top Tips**

o Ponder the gravity of the 'Stranger Burials' sign in Laurel Grove South.

o Try to visit either section of the cemetery first thing in the morning or last thing before they close – the light creates longer shadows for a more atmospheric effect.

o Look for the whipping tree at the center of Laurel Grove South, which still shows lash marks in its bark.

✕ **Take a Break**

Laurel Grove is within easy driving distance of the Historic and Victorian Districts. It's worth it to stop for a bite at one of the many cafes around Starland, such as Foxy Loxy (p129), in between visits to North and South.

Midtown & the Victorian District

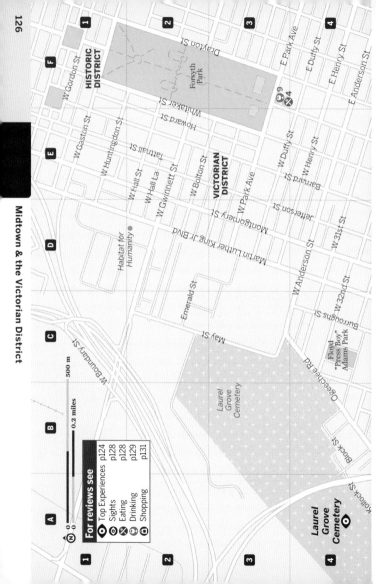

HISTORIC DISTRICT

VICTORIAN DISTRICT

Forsyth Park

W Gordon St

Drayton St

E Park Ave

E Duffy St

E Henry St

E Anderson St

W Gaston St

W Huntingdon St

Tattnall St

Whitaker St

Howard St

W Duffy St

W Henry St

Barnard St

W Hall St
W Hall La
W Gwinnett St
W Bolton St

W Park Ave

Jefferson St

W 31st St

Montgomery St

Habitat for Humanity

Martin Luther King Jr Blvd

W Anderson St

W 32nd St

Emerald St

May St

Burroughs St

Ogeechee Rd

Floyd "Press Boy" Adams Park

Laurel Grove Cemetery

Block St

Laurel Grove Cemetery

Kollock St

W Boundary St

500 m
0.2 miles

For reviews see	
◉ Top Experiences	p124
◎ Sights	p128
✕◎ Eating	p128
◎◎ Drinking	p129
◎ Shopping	p131

Midtown & the Victorian District

Sights

Savannah African Art Museum

MUSEUM

1 ◉ MAP P126, E7

Privately owned museum showcasing more than 1000 19th- and 20th-century spiritual and ceremonial art objects from 22 African countries, with museum volunteers giving guided tours. (☏912-721-7747; visit@savannah africanartmuseum.org; 201 E 37th St; admission free; ◷11am-5pm Wed-Sat)

Daffin Park

PARK

2 ◉ MAP P126, F8

This large recreational park has good walking paths, a pond, lots of grass for sports and picnics, and a public pool. You can catch baseball games at Grayson Stadium, home to the Savannah Bananas baseball team. (☏912-351-3851; 1500 E Victory Dr)

First Friday

ℹ

On the first Friday of each month, galleries, shops and eateries around the Starland Arts District (which loosely radiates out from Bull St, just south of the Victorian District) open their doors for shows, shopping and drinking with local artists and makers.

Sulfur Studios

ART STUDIO

3 ◉ MAP P126, D7

Community art space with a gallery and retail space, plus open artist studios during Starland's First Friday Art March. (www.sulfur studios.org; 2301 Bull St; ◷noon-5pm Thu-Sat)

Eating

Local11Ten

MODERN AMERICAN $$$

4 ✗ MAP P126, F3

Upscale, sustainable, local and fresh: these elements help create an elegant, well-run restaurant that's one of Savannah's best. Start with a blue-crab soufflé, then move on to the seared sea scallops in chive-lemon beurre blanc or the honey and brown-sugar rubbed pork chop and a salted-caramel pot de crème to finish. Wait. Scratch that. The menu already changed.

After dinner, head up to the rooftop bar for a digestif among the oak trees. (☏912-790-9000; www.local11ten.com; 1110 Bull St; mains $26-40; ◷6-10pm; ✗)

Green Truck

PUB FOOD $

5 ✗ MAP P126, F8

Casual pub serving locally sourced and housemade fare (right down to the ketchup). Its burgers are the best in town – we love the Trailer Park, adorned with pimento cheese and bacon. (☏912-234-5885; www.greentruckpub.com; 2430

Habersham St; mains $9-14; ⏱11am-11pm Mon-Sat)

Narobia's Grits & Gravy
BREAKFAST $

6 ✖ MAP P126, F6

Lovers of soul food, seafood and breakfast food will get their fill with the simple, hearty plates at this humble hole in the wall.

The French toast and crab biscuit aren't to be missed. (📞912-231-0563; 2019 Habersham St; ⏱7am-1pm Mon-Fri, to 2pm Sat)

Sweet Spice
JAMAICAN $

7 ✖ MAP P126, E8

This easygoing Jamaican spot, about 4.5 miles southeast of downtown, is a welcome break from all the American and Southern fare you get around here.

A large platter of curry goat or jerk chicken costs just a smidge more than a fast-food meal and it's utterly delicious. It will also keep you filled up for a long time. (📞912-335-8146; www.sweetspice savannah.net; 5515 Waters Ave; mains $6-14; ⏱11am-8pm Mon-Thu, to 9pm Fri & Sat)

Drinking

Foxy Loxy Cafe
CAFE

8 ☕ MAP P126, E6

Buzzing cafe and art-print gallery full of students and creatives set in an old Victorian house. The courtyard out back is the

Laurel Grove Cemetery (p124)

loveliest in this area. It has tasty tacos for when you get peckish, and freshly baked kolaches (fruit pastries) that are positively addictive. There's Sunday brunch, weekday happy hour, and monthly vinyl nights and poetry slams to boot. (📞912-401-0543; www.foxyloxycafe.com; 1919 Bull St; 🕐7am-11pm Mon-Sat, 8am-6pm Sun)

Sentient Bean

CAFE

10 📍 MAP P126, F3

The nightlife in midtown and the Victorian District has a distinctively local flavor, with lots of coffee houses doubling as after-hours hangouts. Sentient Bean is among the best of the bunch, with frequent live music. (📞912-232-4447; www.sentientbean.com; 13 E Park Ave; 🕐7am-9pm; 📶)

Wormhole

BAR

10 📍 MAP P126, D7

This is a locally loved watering hole hosting live bands, comedy, DJs, trivia, open mics, karaoke and more.

There's pool, darts and video games to keep you plenty entertained while you catch a buzz, and it serves a full menu of food until late. (📞912-349-6770; www.wormholebar.com; 2307 Bull St; 🕐noon-3pm Mon-Sat)

Georgia's nickname is the Peach State (p132)

Top Activities 👍

Cooking Classes

When you tire of eating all that sinful Southern food (OK, that may never happen), try your hand at making it – along with dishes from other cuisines – with local top chef Darin Sehnert.

Theme-driven **cooking classes** (Map p126, E8; 📞912-662-6882; www.chefdarinskitchentable.com; 2514 Abercorn St, Suite 40; 4hr class from $75 per person; ⏰11am-6pm Tue-Fri, 10am-6pm Sat) include Low Country Cuisine, French Bistro and Northern Italian. There's also a store stocked with fine kitchen accoutrements.

Volunteering

Help Savannah's needy through **Habitat for Humanity** (Map p126, D2; 📞912-353-8122; www.habitatsavannah.com; 701 Martin Luther King Jr Blvd, ReStore; ⏰9am-5pm Tue-Sat), lending a hand with constructing homes for impoverished residents.

Or help **Old Savannah City Mission** (Map p126, D7; 📞ask for Connell Stiles 912-232-1979; www.oscm.org; 2414 Bull St; ⏰24hr) on a range of tasks.

Shopping

House of Strut   VINTAGE

11 🅐 MAP P126, D7

Our favorite vintage shop in town occupies the sprawling 1st floor of an old Victorian home, where each room is thoughtfully curated with unique, hand-picked fashion finds that are also available for rent.

The space doubles as a venue for local art and music events, and regularly hosts exhibitions, live performances and DJ dance parties. (📞912-712-3902; www.houseofstrut.com; 17 W 41st St, lower unit, ring bell to enter; ⏰11am-7pm Mon-Fri, 10am-6pm Sat, noon-4pm Sun)

Picker Joe's Antique Mall   ANTIQUES

12 🅐 MAP P126, E8

Pickin' and siftin' for antique and vintage treasures is a delight in this bright, clean, organized mall that was once a mattress factory. Military and aviation memorabilia is especially abundant due to owner Jim Plumlee's aviation background, and there's a room dedicated to architectural ornaments and fixtures. (📞912-239-4657; www.pickerjoes.com; 217a E 41st St; ⏰10am-6pm Mon-Sat, noon-5pm Sun)

Soul Food & the African American Diaspora

When it comes to perceptions of cuisine from this part of the country, the distinction between what's known as 'Southern' food and 'soul' food can be blurry.

While all soul food is Southern food, not all Southern food is soul – the roots of the latter stem from what was developed by African slaves in the Southeastern United States as they made do with whatever was available to them. As their descendants migrated north and west during the post-slavery era, they carried the traditional recipes of their forebears with them.

This diaspora brought about what is known today as soul food, a true American immigrant cuisine – in Black communities outside the South, it's a celebration of down-home, rural roots, with traditional dishes being served usually only during special occasions. Typical ones include fried chicken and fish, ham hocks, oxtails, chitlins, pigs' feet, hush puppies and greens (collard, mustard or turnip). These parallel with a lot of Southern foods, though the soul variety is often fattier, saltier and spicier.

Traditionally, soul food wasn't as calorically offensive as we find it today. Its antebellum beginnings were based on seasonally available, organic (before the need for such a term was even a thing) produce, and meat was only used to add flavor to the vegetables. If meat was consumed, it was typically baked or boiled – frying was reserved only for celebratory occasions.

Processed ingredients such as refined flour, sugar and butter were only incorporated on the rare chance they could be obtained. In fact, with such a reliance on dark leafy greens, legumes, root vegetables and seafood, many of today's health fads and diet trends closely resemble early soul-food fare.

Savannah's Year in Food

While the eatin' is good year-round in Savannah, there are particular peaks for fresh produce and the local seafood industry.

May–August: Harvest time for beloved local produce such as Georgia peaches, field peas and okra.

Mid-June: Wild Georgia shrimp are at their biggest and most bountiful until the season comes to a close on December 31.

October–November: It's food and wine festival season, with events taking place almost every weekend.

Georgia's okra and tomatoes

Habersham Antiques Market

ANTIQUES

13 MAP P126, F8

There are plenty of great souvenirs to be found in Savannah, but we think you should snag an opulent chandelier or a Russian egg or some cool '70s cups or...look, whatever you want, really. Someone gave it up in the past, and it's now sold at this market. (912-238-5908; 2502 Habersham St; 9:30am-5:30pm Mon-Fri, 10am-5pm Sat)

Explore ⊕

East Savannah & the Islands

Welcome to a serene side of Savannah where expansive marshlands and winding estuaries slip into the sea. From the city's eastern edge and the riverside township of Thunderbolt, home to Bonaventure Cemetery (p136), past the residential enclaves of Whitemarsh and Talahi Islands, all the way out to the beaches of Tybee Island, great surf, seafood and scenery await by the Atlantic Ocean.

On the way to Tybee Island, you can admire the ramshackle homes along Bonaventure Rd before driving east on US Hwy 80, where you'll cross a tall bridge over the Wilmington River. From here, glowing grasses of the marshes fringe the road, which winds past portals to residential areas and a few shops, where you can grab any last-minute seaside provisions. Continue along Hwy 80 and pop into Fort Pulaski (p141) before crossing the final bridge to Tybee Island. There you'll find eclectic art shops and laid-back beach cafes along Butler Ave.

Getting There & Around

There's only one way on and off these islands. US Hwy 80 threads them all together, starting on the east side of town on Victory Dr, which eventually turns into Butler Ave on Tybee. The bus will only get you as far as Wilmington Island, so if you want to hit the beach, you'll have to go by car.

East Savannah & the Islands Map on p138

Top Experience 📷
Admire the Southern Gothic Necropolis of Bonaventure Cemetery

Nestled on the quiet banks of the Wilmington River, Bonaventure Cemetery is one of the world's most beautiful. Built on a former plantation, the mystical Southern Gothic tombs and monuments, set against a 100-acre natural landscape awash with ferns, azaleas, dwarf palmettos and Spanish-moss-riddled live oaks, conjure a serene reverence that's just the right kind of haunting.

⊙ MAP P138, A2

📞 912-651-6843, Historical Society 912-412-4687

www.bonaventure historical.org

330 Bonaventure Rd

🕗 8am-5pm

🅿

Famous Burials

Bonaventure was the final stop for many well-known Savannahians. Among the most famous grave sites is that of 'Little Gracie' Watson, a six-year-old local girl who died in 1889. Her father had a sculptor carve a detailed, life-sized statue of her from a photograph shortly before the grief-stricken family moved away from Savannah. To this day, visitors bring toys, flowers and other trinkets to her grave.

The cemetery is also home to the grave sites of Great American Songbook-era musician Johnny Mercer, whose family plot features a bench inscribed with lyrics from the singer's works; and Pulitzer Prize-winning poet Conrad Aiken.

Bonaventure in Pop Culture

Bonaventure's beauty became known to the world with the bestselling nonfiction novel and film *Midnight in the Garden of Good and Evil* (John Berendt; 1994). Characters in the book visit the cemetery and gossip over martinis at the grave site of poet Conrad Aiken, where a bench takes the place of a headstone. Scenes from the film, directed by Clint Eastwood, were also shot at the cemetery.

The famous *Midnight* cover features a statue of the *Bird Girl,* which sat virtually unnoticed until 1993 when Random House commissioned local photographer Jack Leigh for an image. After two days of searching for a subject, Leigh quickly captured the photo as dusk approached, then spent 10 hours in the darkroom developing it. The result was an eerie creation that appears awash in moonlight, and it became one of the most iconic photographs ever taken in Savannah. The statue became so popular from the success of the book that it was removed from Bonaventure and now sits on display in the Telfair Academy (p114).

★ **Top Tips**

○ Book the Bonaventure After Hours tour with Bonaventure Cemetery Journeys (p140) for a chance to see the cemetery at night.

○ Bonaventure Historical Society (www.bonaventurehistorical.org) offers free guided afternoon tours one weekend per month – check the website for dates.

○ For self-guided tours, download the Bonaventure Historical Society's Bonaventure Cemetery Tour app.

✕ **Take a Break**

If you're in the mood for a picnic, Bonaventure has a handful of tables on the banks of the river. There are a couple of restaurants in Thunderbolt on River Dr, and in East Savannah off Skidaway Rd. Sisters of the New South (p142) is a great pick if you'd like a little soul food after communing with the dead.

A
B
C
D

1

Savannah River

Elba
Island

Hog
Marsh

2

Goebel Ave

Pennsylvania Ave

Islands Expwy

Savannah

*Bonaventure
Cemetery
Journeys*

Oatland
Island

*Turner
Creek*

Long
Island

McQueens
Island

E Victory Dr

⊗9

◉ **Bonaventure
Cemetery**

80

Johnny Mercer Blvd

**Talahi
Island**

3

Skidaway Rd

Whatley Ave

La Roche Ave

Thunderbolt

**Whitemarsh
Island**

Whitemarsh
Island

Johnny Mercer Blvd

**Wilmington
Island**

4

Herb River

Skidaway River

Wilmington Island Rd

Walthour Rd

Wilmington
Island

Halfmoon River

Isle of Hope

5

Sister
Island

Wilmington River

Cabbage
Island

Skidaway
Island
State Park

204

Diamond
Causeway

McWhorter Dr

Skidaway
Island

6

**Skidaway
Island**

Romerly Marsh Creek

A
B
C
D

East Savannah & the Islands

For reviews see

◉ Top Experiences   p136
◉ Sights   p140
✖ Eating   p141

0 — 5 km
0 — 2.5 miles

E   F   G   H

Fields Cut

New River

Jones Island

Turtle Island

Savannah River

ATLANTIC OCEAN

4 McQueen's Island
◉ Historic Trail

South Channel

Fort Pulaski National Monument

Cockspur Island

◉ **5**

80

Bull River

Tybee Island Light Station & Museum ◉ **3** ◉ **1** North Beach

80

1st St

Tybee Post Theater

✖ **7**

Tybee Island

Tybee Creek

Butler Ave

Little Tybee Island

Little Tybee Creek

Little 2 Tybee ◉ Island

10 ✖ • Tybee Island

✖ **8**
◉ Tybee Pier
6 & Pavilion

ATLANTIC OCEAN

Wassaw Sound

E   F   G   H

Sights

North Beach   BEACH

1 ⊙ MAP P138, H3

With fewer services and a vibe that feels more remote, this stretch of beach is a great place to relax. You can watch massive container ships drift in from sea, especially if you take a left once you hit the sand and walk further north up the shore to the point where the Savannah River runs into the Atlantic. (Railwood Ave, Tybee Island)

Little Tybee Island   ISLAND

2 ⊙ MAP P138, G5

This uninhabited barrier island, only accessible by boat or kayak, is just south of Tybee Island and is actually double its size. The preserved land is rich with coastal marshland, dunes, wildlife and subtropical forests and is a great place to camp. There aren't any facilities on the island, but there's no fee and it's possible to visit any time.

Experienced kayakers can rent from any of the outfitters around Tybee, or book a charter service that runs trips to the island.

Tybee Island Light Station & Museum   LIGHTHOUSE

3 ⊙ MAP P138, H3

Take a self-guided tour of Tybee's iconic lighthouse and see panoramic views of the island from its observation deck. Tickets include admission to the nearby cottage and museum.

It accepts volunteers to greet visitors, interpret and help with on-site projects. Contact Gus Rehnstrom or Art Worden at 912-786-5801 or volunteers@ tybeelighthouse.org. (adult/child $9/7; ◷9am-5:30pm Wed-Mon)

McQueen's Island Historic Trail   WALKING

4 ⊙ MAP P138, E2

This 6-mile walking and biking trail is built over a stretch of the Savannah & Atlantic Railroad line. It parallels the south channel of the Savannah River and you can spot wildlife such as box turtles, red-tailed hawks and brown pelicans.

Cemetery Night Tour

Lovers of history will enjoy **Bonaventure Cemetery Journeys** (Map p138, A2; ☏912-319-5600; www.bonaafter hours.com; 330 Bonaventure Rd; $25-45 per person; ◷day tours 10am & 2pm, night tour 5pm Sat) run by local historian Shannon Scott. The three-hour tour is the only way to see the cemetery at night, offering a different perspective on the history, architecture and traditions of Savannah's alluring city of the dead.

The midpoint entrance is about 15 miles east of Savannah on US Hwy 80 on McQueen's Island, just as soon as you cross the Bull River; park along the road or at Fort Pulaski a little further along. (US Hwy 80, McQueen's Island)

Fort Pulaski National Monument

FORT

5 MAP P138, F3

Located on Cockspur Island at the mouth of the Savannah River, Fort Pulaski was constructed after President James Madison ordered coastal fortifications following the War of 1812. For history buffs, it's worth a stop on the way to Tybee. (www.nps.gov/fopu/index.htm; adult/child under 16 $7/free; ⏱9am-5pm)

Tybee Pier & Pavilion

PIER

6 ⊙ MAP P138, H4

Tybee's main beachside hub, with public bathrooms, concessions and a long fishing pier. Tables in the pavilion are available to rent by the hour. (☏912-652-6780; 16th St at Strand Ave, Tybee Island; ⏱7am-11pm)

Eating

Crab Shack

SEAFOOD $$

7 🍴 MAP P138, G3

This hidden favorite slings bountiful peel-and-eat seafood platters in a multishack complex along an alligator lagoon. Tables have a hole in the center with a giant Rubbermaid trashcan

Fort Pulaski National Monument

underneath, so you know it's legit (don't worry, the cats comin' for your scraps are kempt and dearly beloved members of the family). Get a spot on the patio, if you can. (☎912-786-9857; www. thecrabshack.com; 40 Estill Hammock Rd, Tybee Island; mains $8-25; ⏱11:30am-9pm Sun-Thu, to 10pm Fri & Sat)

Breakfast Club

BREAKFAST $

8 ✖ MAP P138, H4

The line gets long (for a reason) but tables turn quickly at this family-owned breakfast favorite. Staples such as omelets are prepared with fresh ingredients, and they grind their own sausages and burger patties in house; the

Blackhawk breakfast burrito is stellar. (☎912-786-5984; www. thebreakfastclubtybee.com; 1500 Butler Ave, Tybee Island; mains $8-14; ⏱7am-1pm)

Sisters of the New South

SOUTHERN US $

9 ✖ MAP P138, A2

This laid-back cafe beloved of locals serves up Southern soul-food favorites for breakfast, lunch and dinner. The red-velvet cake is among the best we've tried. (☎912-335-2761; www.the sistersofthenewsouth.com; 2605 Skidaway Rd; mains $6-14; ⏱6am-9pm Mon-Thu, to 10pm Fri & Sat, 8am-9pm Sun)

Tybee Island Light Station & Museum (p140)

638138O/GETTY IMAGES ©

Tybee Island

There are several shops on Tybee selling beach essentials – most are located along Butler Ave and on the side streets closer to the south end of the island. There are a few megastores on Whitemarsh and Wilmington Islands, but the options end there.

Nightlife on Tybee Island is limited to a handful of dive bars near the pier, and the occasional performance at the **Tybee Post Theater** (Map p138, H3; ☎912-472-4790; www.tybeeposttheater.org; 10 Van Horne Ave; ☺hours vary by event, check schedule). For a rollicking night out, trek back into town.

Tybee Island Social Club

AMERICAN $$

10 ❌ MAP P138, H4

Inventive starters, burgers, tacos and seafood dishes are best washed down with a signature cocktail at this laid-back haunt. The decor is modern with a touch of rustic, and a bluegrass band plays during brunch. It's a good spot to camp out and enjoy a bottle of wine (if you can nab a parking spot in the tiny front lot). (☎912-472-4044; www.tybeeisland socialclub.com; 1311 Butler Ave, Tybee Island; mains $9-18; ☺noon-10pm Mon-Thu, to midnight Fri & Sat, 11am-10pm Sun)

Worth a Trip 🔭
Discover Wormsloe Historic Site

Known for its iconic corridor of 400 live oak trees that stretch a mile from the entry gate to the main site, the colonial estate of Wormsloe was the first plantation established by the British in Savannah and, over the years, it has served as a military stronghold, a family country residence and a farm.

Getting There

Take Victory Dr east to Skidaway Rd for about 10 miles, then follow the signs; the grand entrance will be on the right.

Wormsloe's Establishment

Thanks to James Oglethorpe's friendship with Yamacraw tribe chief Tomochichi, the uninhabited land that would become Wormsloe was amicably acquired from the native tribe, and in 1737, four years after Savannah was established, the Isle of Hope peninsula was granted to three of the early colonizers. Noble Jones, a carpenter, was among them, and he obtained a lease of 500 acres that would eventually form the core of the site.

Strategic Defense

With establishment in Florida in the previous century, Spain retained loose control over the Georgia coast throughout the late 17th century (thanks to its Native American allies). This brought the Spanish into conflict with the English colonies in the Carolinas.

Their missions off the Georgia coast were subsequently destroyed, rendering the largely abandoned area a buffer zone between the Spanish and the English. When the English opted to colonize the land between Florida and South Carolina – prompting the arrival of Oglethorpe in 1733 – there was concern that the Spanish would attempt to oust them.

Sure enough, conflict broke out with the War of Jenkins' Ear. Wormsloe's strategic location on the Isle of Hope peninsula gave it a valuable role in defending the colony from Spanish attacks from the south. On his 500-acre plot, Jones constructed a fortified house of wood and tabby, a crude concrete composed of oyster shells and lime mortar.

The five-room, 1½-story house featured 8ft ceilings and bastions on all four corners, and was one of several protective outposts along Georgia's chain of barrier islands.

⊙ MAP P27

☐ 912-353-3023; www.gastateparks. org/wormsloe; 7601 Skidaway Rd; adult/ senior/child 6-17yr/ 1-5yr $10/9/4.50/2; ⊙ 9am-5pm daily; P

★ Top Tips

∘ For a dramatic photo op of the Avenue of the Oaks in cooler, damper weather, visit first thing in the morning before the fog dissipates.

∘ Follow the trail through the forest to the Moon River and see Battery Wymberly, military fortifications used during the Civil War.

∘ Two guided tours are offered daily – call ahead to find out which topics will be covered on the day you plan to visit.

∘ On anniversaries of historic dates or holiday weekends, check for special events with costumed demonstrations of colonial-era traditions.

✕ Take a Break

There are picnic tables on site – pack some food.

Survival Guide

Rental bicycles in Charleston (p150) CSFOTOIMAGES/GETTY IMAGES ©

Before You Go

COVID-19 Restrictions

Currently, there are no COVID-related travel restrictions - apart from the requirement for non-US citizens to be vaccinated before entering the country Most businesses in Charleston and Savannah are operating as normal, though some sites may keep shorter hours or require mask-wearing before entering.

Book Your Stay

○ Savannah and Charleston both have a wealth of excellent sleeping options, although budget accommodations are tough to find.

○ Savannah experiences high-season tourism numbers from March to early June, but in the off season – particularly winter months (except for Christmas) – hotel rates can go down by triple digits.

Charleston
°C/°F Temp
Rainfall inches/mm

When to go

Spring and **fall** offer great weather and lots of festivals, drawing in lots of tourists willing to pay top dollar.

Summer is hot and muggy; locals and tourists head for the beach.

Winter is on the chilly side, but you can find good deals on lodgings.

○ Staying in the historic downtown is Charleston's most attractive option, but it's also the most expensive, especially on weekends and in high season.

○ The chain hotels on highways and near Charleston's airport offer significantly lower rates.

Useful Websites

Historic Inns & Boutique Hotels of Savannah (www.bedandbreakfastsofsavannah.com) Info and bookings for six premier Historic District properties.

Mermaid Cottages (www.mermaid cottages.com) Beach cottages and vacation rentals on Tybee.

Historic Charleston B&B (www.historic charlestonbedand breakfast.com) Connects visitors with small homes where owners serve Southern breakfasts and dole out local info.

Lonely Planet (www.lonelyplanet.com/usa/the-south/charleston/hotels) A comprehensive, curated list of hotels.

Best Budget

Thunderbird Inn (www.thethunderbird inn.com) Roadside motel in Savannah with quirky, retro decor.

Not So Hostel (www.notsohostel.com) Charleston's only budget option is creaky, inviting and housed in a wonderful 1840 dwelling.

Savannah Pensione (www.savannahpensione.com) Bare-bones and basic accommodations in an old Victorian house.

Royal Palm Motel (www.royalpalmtybee.com) Budget motel with a tiny pool and an easy walk to Savannah's beachfront.

Best Midrange

Ansonborough Inn (www.ansonboroughinn.com) An intimate Historic District hotel in Charleston with the vibe of an antique sailing ship.

Indigo Inn (www.indigoinn.com) Snazzy boutique inn right in the middle of Charleston's Historic District.

1837 Bed & Breakfast (www.1837bb.com) Charmingly over decorated inn near the College of Charleston.

East Bay Inn (www.eastbayinn.com) Traditionally furnished rooms in a historic Savannah inn.

River Street Inn (www.riverstreetinn.com) Waterfront inn housed in a former 19th-century cotton warehouse in Savannah.

Atlantis Inn (www.atlantisinntybee.com) Quaint rooms in Savannah with quirky murals and funky fixtures.

Best Top End

Kimpton Brice (www.bricehotel.com) Hip, ecofriendly boutique hotel in Savannah, with contemporary design elements.

Mansion on Forsyth Park (www.mansiononforsythpark.com) Opulent and sprawling Savannah mansion with views of Forsyth Park.

Beachview Bed & Breakfast (www.beachviewbbtybee.com) Laid-back, colorful and charming B&B a short walk from Savannah's beach.

Wentworth Mansion (www.wentworthmansion.com) A Gilded Age Charleston mansion loaded up with Tiffany stained-glass and hand-carved mahogany moldings.

Zero George Street (www.zerogeorge.com) Restored, circa-1804 stucco Charleston home with a fabulous restaurant.

Restoration (www.therestorationhotel.com) Boutique hipster enclave in Charleston, steeped in Americana arts-and-crafts kitsch.

Arriving in Charleston & Savannah

Charleston International Airport

Getting downtown from **Charleston International Airport** (Map p82, D1; ☎ 843-767-7009; www.chs-airport.com; 5500 International Blvd) is easy and fast with shuttles, taxis, buses, ridesharing and a rental-car center at your service. The airport is about 10 miles from the center of the city.

Savannah/ Hilton Head International Airport

From **Savannah/ Hilton Head International Airport** (📞912-964-0514; www. savannahairport.com; 400 Airways Ave), rent a car, call a rideshare or catch a taxi to the Historic District for $28. Chatham Area Transit (CAT) operates the 100X Airport Express route ($8 return) between the airport and the **JMR Intermodal Transit Center** (610 W Oglethorpe Ave) downtown.

Greyhound

Savannah's Greyhound Station (Map p112, A2; 📞 912-232-2135; www.greyhound.com; 610 W Oglethorpe Ave) sits right on the edge of the Historic District, and you can

walk to your accommodations from here or catch a rideshare or metered taxi.

Charleston's Greyhound Station (Map p82, E1; 📞 843-744-4247; www.greyhound.com; 3610 Dorchester Rd) is in North Charleston, and it's simple to take a rideshare downtown. There's also a CARTA bus stop (route 11) in front of the station.

Amtrak

Savannah's Amtrak Station (Map p112, A4; www.amtrak.com; 2611 Seaboard Coastline Dr) is a few miles from the Historic District. Call a rideshare or metered taxi.

Charleston's Amtrak Station (Map p82, E1; www.amtrak.com; 4565 Gaynor St) is in North Charleston, and taking a rideshare from here is simple. The adjacent CARTA bus stop (route 10) will also get you to the downtown area.

Getting Around

Bicycle

Charleston's flat terrain is ideal for bicycling. There are plenty of racks around town, and activists have been successful in getting some bike lanes and trails added.

Holy Spokes (Map p64, D4; 📞843-270-5346; https://charlestonbikeshare. com; 7 Radcliffe St, Suite 200; per hour/day $8/12; ⏱24hr) is the city bikeshare plan, with 27 locations downtown.

A great rental place for longer periods is **Affordabike** (Map p64, D4; 📞843-789-3281; http://affordabike.com; 573 King St; per day/week $25/55; ⏱10am-6pm Mon-Sat, noon-5pm Sun).

Boat

Charleston Water Taxi (📞 843-330-2989; www.charlestonwatertaxi. com; 10 Wharfside St; day pass adult/child $12/10; ⏱9am-8pm mid-Mar–mid-Nov, 10am-6pm Sat rest of the year) offers ferry service around Charleston Harbor, with stops at the aquarium, Patriot's Point in Mt Pleasant, the Charleston Harbor Marina and Waterfront Park. You can buy tickets online or on the boat.

There's also an Uber-style app for boats, called **HOBA** (www.hobarides.com). We're told it's a great way to get out on the water.

The free **Savannah Belles Ferry** (www.catchacat.org), designed in an old riverboat ferry style, connects downtown with Hutchinson Island across the Savannah River. It has the following stops:

o River St at City Hall.

o Waving Girl Landing at the Savannah Marriott Riverfront Hotel.

o Hutchinson Island at the Savannah International Trade & Convention Center.

Bus

CARTA (☎ 843-724-7420; www.ridecarta.com) runs city-wide buses around Charleston; the one-way cash fare is $2. **DASH Trolley** (☎ 843-202-4410; www.charlestoncvb.com/blog/know-dash; ⊙ schedules vary) has free streetcars that do three loop routes from the visitor center.

Savannah's Chatham Area Transit (www.catchacat.org) operates local buses that run on bio-diesel, including a free shuttle (the dot) that makes its way around the Historic District and stops near most major sights.

Car & Motorcycle

Most major car-rental companies, such as

Avis (☎ 843-767-7030; www.avis.com; ⊙6am-midnight), have offices at Charleston International Airport. Be warned: parking is an issue. City parking lots charge around $2 per hour, and many hotels charge upward of $20 a night for parking.

Beyond the Historic and Victorian Districts of Savannah, transportation by car is the easiest means of getting around. Motorcycles are also seen citywide.

Taxi

Ridesharing apps are typically cheaper and easier than call-

Tipping

Tipping is *not* optional; only withhold tips in cases of outrageously bad service.

Restaurant servers 18% to 20%, unless a gratuity is already charged on the bill (usually only for groups of six or more).

Bartenders 15% to 20% per round, minimum per drink $1 standard drinks, $2 specialty cocktail.

Taxi drivers 10% to 15%, rounded up to the next dollar.

Hotel porters $2 per bag, minimum per cart $5.

Hotel maids $2 to $4 per night, left in envelope or under the card provided.

ing or finding a taxi, and many locals get around this way.

Essential Information

Accessible Travel

These cities are generally pretty friendly to travelers with disabilities, as most businesses are in compliance with ADA regulations, and ramps and elevators are available at most multilevel sights. That said, the uneven sidewalks and alleyways aren't great for wheelchairs.

There's free parking for people with disabilities in government-run parking areas.

Download Lonely Planet's free Accessible Travel guides from http://lptravel.to/AccessibleTravel.

Business Hours

Opening hours vary throughout the year. We provide high-season opening hours; hours will generally decrease in the shoulder and low seasons.

Banks 9am-5pm Mon-Fri

Restaurants 9am-10pm

Cafes 7am-7pm

Bars and clubs 5pm-2am

Shops 10am-6pm

Discount Cards

In both Savannah and Charleston, numerous sightseeing tour companies offer a range of packages with access to top sights. Visit kiosks around the cities' historic districts for coupons to individual attractions.

Electricity

Type A
120V/60Hz

Type B
120V/60Hz

Money

ATMs are widespread, and credit cards are widely accepted.

Public Holidays

Major holidays and special events may mean many businesses are closed, or may attract crowds, making dining and accommodations reservations difficult.

New Year's Day January 1

Martin Luther King Jr Day Third Monday in January

Presidents' Day Third Monday in February

Dos & Don'ts

Savannahians and Charlestonians ooze Southern charm and politeness. Don't be alarmed by people wanting to chat to you and learn your life story – and tell you theirs.

Greetings Handshakes are common when meeting men and women for the first time. Say 'hello' and 'goodbye' to staff when visiting shops, restaurants and sights.

Taboo topics It may be best to keep thoughts on US politics to yourself – you never know who you might offend. Also, Christian culture is overt; tread conscientiously with topics relating to religion.

Sensitivity about race These cities were centers of the slave trade, and places connected with that history should be treated with respect. For instance, when touring Charleston's Old Slave Mart Museum, it is not funny or OK to ask where you can get yourself a slave. (People have actually done this.)

St Patrick's Day March 17

Easter March/April

Memorial Day Last Monday in May

Independence Day July 4

Labor Day First Monday in September

Halloween October 31

Thanksgiving Fourth Thursday in November

Christmas Day December 25

New Year's Eve December 31

Responsible Travel

◦ Reduce your carbon footprint. Opt for trains and buses rather than planes if practical. Where possible, take public transportation and explore on foot or bicycle rather than car.

◦ Reduce waste Use a refillable water bottle rather than buying single-use plastic. Carry and use your own bag when making purchases.

◦ Buy local. Shop at farmers markets, seek out locally owned restaurants and buy crafts straight from the source. Find trusted local businesses at www.buylocalsavannah.com and www.lowcountrylocalfirst.org.

◦ Avoid overtourism. Try to travel outside of peak season (generally March to May and September to October); visit major sights on weekdays rather than weekends.

◦ Be kind. Southerners are generally polite to a fault. Be sure you give greetings when entering or leaving a business.

Safe Travel

Charleston is a safe city with a relatively low crime rate, but dangerous and violent crime is a reality in Savannah, with one of the highest rates in the US.

◦ Be vigilant and avoid walking alone at night in areas where there aren't a lot of people. That said, robberies have been known to happen in Savannah in broad daylight, even in parts of downtown with heavy tourist traffic.

○ Don't leave valuables in vehicles in Savannah, as car break-ins and theft happen frequently.

Toilets

There are very few public restroom facilities in Savannah. Find them at Ellis Sq, the Bryan St and Liberty St parking garages, the Visitors Center on MLK Blvd and the River St Hospitality Center. The best public bathroom in Charleston is inside Charleston Place.

Tourist Information

Savannah Visitors Center (Map p112, B4; 📞 912-944-0455; www.savannahvisit.com; 301 Martin Luther King Jr Blvd; ⏰ 9am-5:30pm) Excellent resources and services are available in this center, which is based in a restored 1860s train station. Many privately operated city tours start here. There is also a small, interactive tourist-info kiosk in the visitor center at Forsyth Park.

Charleston Visitor Center (📞 843-724-7174; www.charlestoncvb.com; 375 Meeting St; ⏰ 8:30am-5:30pm Apr-Oct, to 5pm Nov-Mar) Find help with accommodations and tours or watch a half-hour video on Charleston history in this spacious renovated warehouse.

North Charleston Visitor Center (Map p82, E1; 📞 843-853-8000; www.charlestoncvb.com; 4975b Centre Point Dr; ⏰ 10am-5pm Mon-Sat, 1-5pm Sun) Has brochures, maps and staff who can help you plan your trip.

Index

See also separate subindexes for:

⊗ **Eating** p157

◉ **Drinking** p158

✪ **Entertainment** p158

⊜ **Shopping** p158

Sights 000

Map Pages **000**

Behind the Scenes

Send Us Your Feedback

We love to hear from travelers – your comments help make our books better. We read every word, and we guarantee your feedback goes straight to the authors. Visit **lonelyplanet.com/contact** to submit your updates and suggestions. Note: We may edit, reproduce and incorporate your comments in Lonely Planet products such as guidebooks, websites and digital products, so let us know if you are happy to have your name acknowledged. For a copy of our privacy policy visit **lonelyplanet.com/legal**.

Ashley's Thanks

Many thanks to Erin Morris, Kourtnay King, Paul Haynes, Chandler Routman, Jason, Elizabeth, Iris and Loulou Ryan, Patty Pascal, Halsey Perrin, Kim Jamieson, Ruta Fox, and Chris Dorsel.

MaSovaida's Thanks

Many thanks to the lovely souls in Savannah and beyond who provided tips and guidance, Chad Faries, Emily Jones, Robert Firth, Trisha Ping, Ny, Ty and Haj.

Acknowledgements

Cover photograph: Savannah riverfront promenade, Sean Pavone/Shutterstock ©

Back cover photograph: Wormsloe, Serge Skiba/Shutterstock ©

Photographs pp 26-27 (clockwise from left): Cvandyke/Shutterstock ©; Leamus/Getty Images ©; f11photo/Shutterstock ©; Larry Knupp/Shutterstock ©; aimintang/Getty Images ©; northforklight/Getty Images ©; Gordon Bell/Shutterstock ©; Aaron Hyslop/Shutterstock ©

This Book

This 2nd edition of Lonely Planet's *Pocket Charleston & Savannah* guidebook was written by Ashley Harrell, MaSovaida Morgan and Regis St Louis. The previous edition was written by Ashley and MaSovaida. This guidebook was produced by the following:

Destination Editor Trisha Ping

Senior Product Editors Kate Chapman, Vicky Smith, Kate Mathews

Product Editors Sarah Farrell, Sam Wheeler

Cartographers Julie Sheridan, Alison Lyall

Book Designers Mazzy Prinsep, Gwen Cotter

Assisting Editors Nigel Chin, Victoria Harrison, Alexander Knights, Kellie Langdon

Cover Researchers Hannah Blackie, Naomi Parker

Thanks to Ronan Abayawickrema, Alex Conroy, Sonia Kapoor, Sandie Kestell, Angela Tinson, Amanda Williamson

Our Writers

Ashley Harrell

Ashley went to journalism grad school, convinced a newspaper to hire her, and started covering wildlife, crime and tourism. Fueling her zest for storytelling and the unknown, she traveled widely and moved often, from a vast California ranch to a jungle cabin in Costa Rica, where she started writing for Lonely Planet.

MaSovaida Morgan

MaSovaida is a Lonely Planet writer and multi-media storyteller whose wanderlust has taken her to more than 35 countries across six continents. She was Lonely Planet's Destination Editor for South America for four years and worked as an editor for newspapers and NGOs in the Middle East and the United Kingdom. Follow her on Instagram @MaSovaida.

Regis St Louis

Regis grew up in a small American Midwest town and developed a fascination with foreign dialects and world cultures. He learned Russian and a handful of Romance languages, which served him well on journeys across much of the globe. Regis has contributed to more than 50 Lonely Planet titles, across six continents. Follow him on Instagram @regisstlouis.

Published by Lonely Planet Global Limited
CRN 554153
2nd edition – Dec 2022
ISBN 978 1 78701 752 8
© Lonely Planet 2022   Photographs © as indicated 2022
10 9 8 7 6 5 4 3 2 1
Printed in Singapore